Setting YourSelf Free

Setting YourSelf Free

Breaking the Cycle of Emotional Abuse in Family, Friendships, Work and Love

SaraKay Smullens, MSW, LCSW, BCD

New Horizon Press
Far Hills, New Jersey

New Horizon Press
P.O. Box 669
Far Hills, NJ 07931

In writing this book the author found the following work invaluable:
Eli Marcovitz, M.D., "Dignity," *Bulletin of the Philadelphia Association for
Psychoanalysis*, Vol. XX, No. 2 (June 1970)

Cover Design: Robert Aulicino
Interior Design: Susan M. Sanderson
Illustrations: Megan Nelson
Author Photo: Sharon J. Wohlmuth

Library of Congress Control Number: 2002101392

Smullens, SaraKay
    Setting YourSelf Free: Breaking the Cycle of Emotional Abuse in Family,
    Friendships, Work and Love

ISBN: 0-88282-224-1
New Horizon Press

Manufactured in the U.S.A.

2006   2005   2004   2003   2002 / 5   4   3   2   1

To Stanton

who was first a friend, who cared for and loved Elisabeth and
Kathyanne and who brought Liz and Doug into my life.

And then the magic began...

"...and yes I said yes I will Yes."

James Joyce, *Ulysses*

AUTHOR'S NOTE

This book is based on my counseling work with clients, their real life experiences and my own experience in coping with emotional abuse. Fictitious names and identities have been given to all clients in the book in order to protect individual confidentiality. This book is not intended to replace necessary therapy with mental health professionals.

TABLE OF CONTENTS

PREFACE

My Cycle Begins

In my own life, the cycle of emotional abuse began early in child-hood, but it was not until many years later that I was able to iden-tify and deal with the lingering legacy of that cycle within which I was trapped. In addition to stories from my clients, I have used stories from my personal life in this book, because I want to demonstrate my belief that people, no matter what they have suffered, can grow and change. The real criteria is that they can do this **if and only if** they are brave enough to face reality. (Please note: my personal experience is reproduced in italics).

My mother died at 3:00 A.M. on April 10, 1995—the morning of my birthday—after valiantly fighting cancer for three years. That morning, at 2:45 A.M., I suddenly awakened at home feeling unable to catch my breath. I tele-phoned my mother's hospice room. A nurse held the telephone to my mother's ear as I thanked her for being with me for one more birthday. Later the nurse told me that after I had spoken with her for the last time, my mother's eyes brimmed with tears as she smiled and whispered, "To be continued."

For many years, my mother had been saddened and guilty, because when I was three-and-a-half years old, she had become too emotionally disturbed to care for me and had to send me to live with relatives nearby in Baltimore. Afterward, she described those years as a complete blur. The professional help she needed was not offered, but by the time I was six-and-a-half years old she had improved enough for me to return home. She and my father bought a house in the suburbs and we left my beloved downtown Baltimore forever. I was happy to be with my mother once again, but forever afterward missed the loving relatives and wonderfully diverse cityscape neighborhood that had been kind to me and good for me.

The first winter after our move, my mother became pregnant with my sister. Our new home was never to be a stable or joyful one. However, there were some moments of happiness and I took comfort in the depth of the relationship between my mother and me. We shared an enduring and profound love, in spite of everything that remained difficult throughout my childhood.

I know now how ill both of my parents were, but as a child and even as a teenager, I had no understanding of my mother's terrifying mood swings or my father's withdrawal and rage. I believe with all of my heart that with professional help, my mother would have been able to leave my father and find a more stable and satisfying life. However, times were different then; there was a terrible stigma attached to psychological help (In some circles, this attitude remains.). Women had very few options: College education was mostly limited to wealthy and privileged women. Most professional doors were barely opened. There were "married" women and "career" women. The latter were usually social pariahs. These were the years when little girls played the card game "Old Maid"—no one wanted to be stuck with that horrid card in real life.

And so, given the times and given her options, my mother turned all her frustration, hurt and anger inward for as long as she could. When she could bear it no longer, she exploded verbally, violently—usually toward me. Her explosions, I now know, were cries for help. I heard them, but had no power, no ability to help.

When my mother was feeling well, she loved to talk about theater, dance, film and politics. She had a wonderful sense of humor and during these times her conversation was filled with laughter. Her husband did not join in; he was consistently quiet, sullen and petulant at home. But to outsiders, his behavior was always warm, gregarious and charming. Through the years friends would tell me, "You're lucky—your dad is so handsome and so much fun. He really loves to have a good time!"

One evening, when I was about ten years old, I came home from school to find my mother sobbing. I prepared dinner and gave my screaming three-year-old sister a bath, warming the water that had been run for her hours before. Then I put my mother to bed. When my father came home, hours later than he was expected and with no explanation as to why, I told him that something was terribly wrong with my mother and asked him to please help her. He responded by screaming at me for not being helpful enough to her. He called me spoiled, selfish and stupid and said that he hated me so much he wished I had never been born. Then he put his coat on and left.

In her own way, my mother tried desperately to get help. When no one heard her words or her screams, her body started screaming for her. It rebelled. She somatized, meaning that she displaced her emotional trauma onto her body and consulted her doctor about endless physical problems: she hurt all the time, she confided. Unable to find anything wrong, her doctor, a kind man who was determined to help, responded by sending her to a surgeon. My mother had surgery after surgery, all completely unnecessary, none of which mended her broken heart or her terror of my father's wrath. Later came the cancer.

A few weeks after my mother died, I awakened from a sound sleep, again at 2:45 A.M. Only half-awake, I dreamed that I heard my mother's voice, urging me to finish my personal journal.

On that evening, my journal already contained well over a thousand pages. Yet not until then did I recognize that the account I had written of my life was far from complete. I began to see that although I had kept a faithful record of events, I had not fully understood them.

For the next eighteen months—on unpredictable days, but always just before 3:00 A.M.—I awakened and returned to the room where my journal laid. In rereading my journal, I gradually learned to truly understand the advice that I now offer to each of those who meet with me in my office to seek counseling: old wounds heal slowly and are not easily forgotten. However, acknowledging that these wounds are part of us and part of our successful struggle to survive in spite of everything will make us stronger and wiser, because in recognizing these wounds, we are armored and can protect ourselves against new injuries.

For each of us, this process—learning to heal the injuries of the past so that we can enjoy the present to its fullest measure of happiness—is one that continues. And this process is and will remain the only way to end the malignant cycle of emotional abuse.

ACKNOWLEDGMENTS

Through the years of writing this book there have been several friends and colleagues who have studied my work and offered invaluable guidance, direction and support.

I will never find appropriate words of thanks for Blanche Schlessinger, my extraordinary literary agent and close friend, who believed in this book from its inception, offered hundreds of hours of guidance and found exactly the right publisher.

My gratitude to Laurie Graham, my unparalleled editor of *Whoever Said Life is Fair?* and treasured friend; to Robbin Reynolds, my first literary agent who believes deeply in my first book and guided me back to journal writing in 1982 in order to prepare to write this one. It is also important to thank Tom Wark and Bill Stroud of the *Philadelphia Inquirer*, who hired me during my years as a single parent, nurtured my ability to write and believed in my talents. I also thank my many readers who continue to speak of columns that they found meaningful. And my thanks to Don Harrison and Michael Schefer of the *Philadelphia Daily News* and John Timpane of the *Philadelphia Inquirer* who have continued to offer opportunities to use insights from my work to comment on social and political issues.

The kindnesses, guidance and encouragement of Carl Brandt and Margaret Maycumber through many years will not be forgotten.

My deep gratitude to early supporters of my writing for their continued friendship and many acts of presence and caring, including Marciarose Shestack and Bonnie Strauss, who encouraged me to write in order to increase my income as a single parent, Sonia

Woldow, Nancy Glazer, Margot Horwitz, Geraldine Deitz Fox and Michael Bayleson, Esq., the first person in my life to call me a writer.

My heartfelt thanks to Sharon Nelson, Richard Mandel, Patty Freed, Joan Brucker, Dr. Faith Bethelard, Marie Field, Margo Howard, Reverend Leonard Thompson, Bonnie Kane, Mimi Rose, Judith Stalberg Friedman, Gloria Hochman, Fusako Yokobori, Belle Parmet, Dr. Yoram (Jerry) and Dina Wind, Dr. Hugh Rosen and Gene Dilks, Esq. who offered to read my manuscript and provided invaluable advice, guidance, friendship and time as they studied my work and helped me improve its direction and quality.

A deep and lasting thank you to Nancy Steele, who worked closely and patiently with me as we translated several hundred pages into a suitable manuscript for submission. My debt is also enormous to my wise and wonderful friend, Stuart Horwitz, who painstakingly and dedicatedly assisted in the creation of this final version.

Deep appreciation to Dr. Joan Dunphy, the President of New Horizon Press and my editor, for her wise and committed guidance and belief that this book can and will help others. My grateful thanks also both to Lynda Hatch, Assistant Editor, Acquisitions and Development, who assisted in editing and whose support, patience and belief in this project have been invaluable and to Rebecca Sheil, Assistant Editor/Production Manager, who did the final editing with enormous care and kindness.

To my able assistant and friend, Linda Rebstock, words cannot express my thanks. Also grateful thanks to my friend Willie Mae Washington, who typed the initial manuscript of *Whoever Said Life Is Fair?* and did countless work on this manuscript as well, and to Mary McMonigle, Marianne Anthony and Jennifer Panaccio, who helped and supported in myriad ways.

My gratitude to the University of Pennsylvania School of Social Work, where I learned to understand human behavior through art, drama, painting and history. Here I began to see how to free clients' potentials and help them soar.

While a young clinician at Philadelphia Psychiatric Hospital, the late Dr. Morris Brody invited me to participate in course work available to psychiatric residents and Marvin Greenberg invited me to train and participate in early work in family therapy. I remain indebted to both.

Deep and heartfelt thanks to the late Dr. Eli Marcovitz, who offered unrestricted use of his papers "Dignity" and "Aggression in Human Adaptation" for my work so that readers could benefit from his hard-won insights on dignity, shame, humiliation, pride, humility and aggression. He insisted on no recognition whatsoever for the gifts or his words and insights, but I believe it is his due. I will forever remain enormously grateful for his gifts of availability, friendship and mentoring.

My most profound thanks are for my husband and children, but words alone could never adequately express my debt. Surely it would be impossible to fully thank Liz, Elisabeth, Doug and Kathyanne for all of the support they have given through my years of work. My previous book was dedicated to Elisabeth and Kathyanne.

I cannot imagine a personal world without Liz and Doug, who came into my life at ages twelve and nine. Blending our two families was hard work on everyone's part, but when I saw Liz and Doug I was blessed with a feeling of "love at first sight."

My eternal love and gratitude go to my husband, Stanton, for his indescribable acts of caring and presence; his help with this manuscript (and the many attempts—too many to count—that preceded it) as I struggled to say what was deep within me; and his constant (and almost always patient) availability each time my computer and I stopped communicating. I can say unequivocally that the only person happier than I that this book is finally completed is my husband.

Stan and I both thank our cherished first grandchild, Charlotte Rose, who bears my mother's name, for her magic and the exquisite hope of her presence.

SaraKay Smullens
Philadelphia, Pennsylvania
January 26, 2002

INTRODUCTION

The Cycle
of Emotional Abuse

Though we now know we live in a world threatened by malevolent outside dangers, there also exists a danger within, an invisible, expanding pestilence—unseen and unrealized by most people. This scourge is threatening the stability of our families and the future health of our children. It is emotional abuse. If you think you and your loved ones are immune to this infestation, think again! Some families appear respected, close, secure and loving in the world outside of the home, while a step inside their homes when no one is looking will reveal the presence of insults, blame, ridicule, lies and humiliation. In such families, members are coerced by "the silent treatment," threats, intimidation and bullying—all powerful but invisible weapons of psychological attack that inflict deep and lasting wounds.

Within the family is where the decay of emotional abuse first appears. However, even if your home is one where there is trust and respect, you and your family members may venture forth into the world and meet professional acquaintances, love interests, friends, fellow employees or bosses who come from these afflicted backgrounds and use emotional abuse to gain their ends. You may become entrapped and seduced by them, much more easily than people realize.

Why does an individual become emotionally abusive? It has nothing to do with wealth and everything to do with family and society. A person without the opportunity to learn to think rationally—one who is rejected and ignored by a parent, lashed out upon with hate or ridicule or is dominated or overly indulged—does not develop a sense of autonomy. Though such individuals often mask it brilliantly, they do not develop the strength to navigate life's slippery slopes or the confidence to deal with overwhelming feelings of inadequacy, jealousy and envy. Once grown-up, the only way they know how to live is to control others, often skillfully as well as charismatically. Such people live by finding scapegoats (usually their partners, children, co-workers) and projecting their impotent rage upon them. In order to function, emotionally abusive individuals do everything in their power to keep their family members, lovers, friends and colleagues from creating happy homes and lives for themselves.

Young children are at the root of the emotional abuse cycle. They are especially susceptible to an inability to match their own perceptions against those of the outside world. They long for their parents to love them. They feel dependent on them for the very air they breathe. They take parental words as gospel; their parents' needs are holy expectations. And so, when these children see emotional abuse or when they feel it expressed toward themselves or others they may love, they silence the tiny voice within that tries to warn them by speaking the truth. They do so for one reason: fear. Emotionally abused children believe if they allow themselves to see and be conscious of how they are being treated, they will lose their abusive parents' love and without it, they will die.

"The scars are all on the inside, the voice of truth is buried within," is an axiom that we in the mental health field say and believe. Often you never know who are victims of emotional abuse until their behavior results in alcoholism or a drug or sexual addiction (*voice of truth*: "This is the only way I can numb my pain and get release and relief"); eating disorders (*voice of truth*: "Things are eating me up alive and I am acting out with food, putting my life in jeopardy as I do so. Down deep I know it's not what I am eating, but what's eating me. But I am too scared to face it"); physical illnesses that have no discernible cause, such as unexplainable urinary tract pain (*voice of truth*: "I'm pissed, but I won't let myself feel it, so my body is acting it out"); constant skin eruptions, such as boils, that do not respond to treatment (*voice of truth*: "I am boiling, but cannot say so"); stomach disorders (*voice of truth*: "There are things I can't stomach, but I can't allow myself to know it and say it out loud, so my body is answering for me"); and even suicide (*voice of truth*: "I am in so much pain that I cannot make a distinction between myself and my pain. The only way to end the pain is to end my own life").

I have seen emotional abuse up close as a therapist. I have worked with children whose parents claim they love them and yet do everything in their power to destroy their children's opportunities, their attempts at expression, their individuality and their confidence. I have seen husbands who claim their marriages are excellent, even as they coldly withhold affection from their wives while flaunting sexual interest in others, culminating in some cases in torturous public affairs. I have seen women consistently insult and demean husbands, ensuring through these actions that the men remain in an infantilized or subordinate state. I have seen families viewed as benevolent and kind treat the sick and old in their homes with cruelty and contempt. I have seen bullies in the workplace make their subordinates feel so uncomfortable that they become ill or so angry and helpless that they become violent.

In almost every case, the abusers claim to be doing the opposite of what their treatment of others and actions indicate. What they say has absolutely nothing to do with what they actually mean and do! The victims of emotional abusers—children, friends, lovers, co-workers and partners—are forever caught in relentless, crazy-making mazes. They either begin to accept the abusive treatment and the lies disguised as truths—or they are punished. In time, if the abused don't find ways out of the mazes, by finding the strength to face reality as well as see and understand the truth about what is happening to them, they will continue to be victims in relationship after relationship, with friends, lovers, co-workers, partners and their own children. Or they themselves will become emotional abusers.

Emotional abuse can be as destructive as physical and sexual violence. Abusers who practice psychological manipulation, financial control and social isolation can paralyze their victims, depriving them of their independence and self-esteem and destroying their happiness, careers and health. Often, an act of emotional abuse can be preceded or followed by acts of physical or sexual abuse. There is frequently a coexistence of more than one of these three types of injuries. However, because it is invisible, difficult to detect and rarely explained or identified in day-to-day life—and because it relentlessly threatens the very fabric of healthy and enduring relationships—I have chosen in this book to focus exclusively on emotional abuse.

Why is emotional abuse often the hidden member among this trio of emotional, physical and sexual abuse? Let's take social isolation as an example. Social isolation is a form of emotional abuse that separates its victims from families and friends, sometimes by physical relocation to unfamiliar areas. Without emotional support from families and friends, these victims become increasingly vulnerable. Individuals whose partners are very jealous and controlling may become prisoners in their own homes. In time, some abusers become able to control their victims' perceptions of the abuse and victims may begin to doubt their own sanity. This inability to trust their own feelings can be compounded by the ways the abusers present themselves to the outside world. Emotional abusers may carefully mind their manners in public and practice abuse only in private, lashing out with vicious verbal attacks or false accusations when they're least expected.

The psyche is a closed system. Very often depression is anger turned inward. When the anger that results from being a victim of emotional abuse is turned inward, it often manifests in self-destructive behaviors. It may also determine the types of relationships we choose and the cycles that we allow to continue and, in some cases, prevail. The horrific wounds of emotional abuse do not stop hurting when we turn eighteen or twenty-one. When emotional abuse begins in childhood within the family, it leaves us vulnerable to and possibly entrapped in future emotional abusive relationships with friends, lovers, life partners and co-workers, thus forming an ever-expanding cycle of emotional abuse.

There are many, many different definitions of the word "cycle" throughout the various sciences. In astronomy, a cycle is the orbit of a planet that recurs every set number of years. In physics, it is called "the curve of binding energy," which describes the way that something that has been put into motion creates its own future, like a self-fulfilling prophecy. In mechanics, a cycle refers to a recurrent series of states, in an engine for example.

The basic idea of a cycle is that the form remains the same, while the content changes. A cycle is something that repeats with fresh material: A boy who is verbally abused by his father may feel comfortable in a workplace with a verbally abusive boss, for example. The boy, who is now a man, at least externally, may even seek out such an environment, because it feels familiar. At the very least, he may not have the will to leave his oppressive employer, because the cycle has caused him to regress to an age at which he cannot assert himself.

My favorite definition of a cycle comes from botany, the science of flowers, plants and trees. In the world of plants, a natural, healthy cycle begins as a series of leaves in a circle, a "whorl" as it is called, that is exactly mirrored by another series of leaves above it (see Figure 1).

Without knowing it, victims of emotional abuse, instead of experiencing a healthy birth and growth cycle, experience a formative cycle of diseased mutation. They pass from the blighted experiences in their childhood, directly into other dysfunctional experiences of friendship, romantic partnership or even their general attitude toward the world, simply because it feels natural to do so. As in a blighted botanical cycle, the new experiences of human beings will "mirror" their original abusive experience.

The first chapter of this book details the roots of emotional abuse, showing the various types that may be suffered at the hands of one's parents or caretakers. The next two chapters detail how the "style" of emotional abuse that you suffered affects your relationships with siblings and later with friends. Chapter 4 shows how this emotional

Figure 1

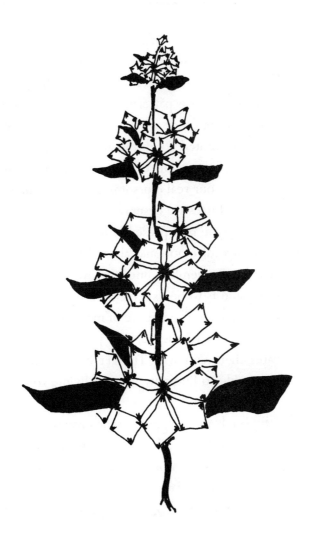

Figure 2

abuse plays itself out so frequently and powerfully in your love and marriage relationships. Chapter 5 connects the effect of emotional abuse on your experience in the workplace, while chapter 6 details how emotional abuse colors your interactions within the community and society at large.

Returning to the metaphor of healthy and blighted plants used earlier, it is easy to see the diseased "flowering" of emotional abuse (see Figure 2) through the various stages and ages of the life of an emotional abuse victim. In diseased plants, these flowers are not the beautiful and aromatic flowers which most of us picture. They are more like what Baudelaire called, "flowers of evil." The blighted blossoms reflect that playing out the patterns of emotional abuse may seem natural, organic even, but they are not. It is only when we look closely, perceive the deteriorated condition and find the courage to prune the diseased parts of the plant, that we can break the pattern of emotional abuse, achieve our real blossoming and find the healthy, sustaining relationships and lives we deserve.

Realizing that the way you may presently be acting in your life is dictated by the experience of emotional abuse in childhood should not be a cause for shame. Remember, until the cycle is stopped, this appears normal to you and is to be expected. However, the cycle of emotional abuse can be broken. The science of my profession involves understanding the behaviors of the various people with whom I work, what motivates them and why. The art lies in buffering the attacked until they are able to find new ways of living, free of emotional abuse.

Think of using this book as your guide to the growth of awareness as well as your buffer. To end the cycle of emotional abuse, it is necessary to face painful realities. This book will illustrate how to confront emotional injuries, how to place the past in perspective, how to avoid needless pain and how to recognize opportunities for happiness.

In chapters 7 through 9 of this book, I will show you how, once you have identified the particular cycle or combination of cycles of emotional abuse in which you may be trapped, you can start to heal in all of your important relationships. Everyone has a natural inner voice that helps guide toward positive experiences and warns against destructive and abusive ones. Yours has been stilled, but not silenced. However, by the time you get to chapter 7, your inner voice will be far more accessible to you. In emotionally abusive homes one learns to push down this voice, refusing to hear its alarming message. I will show you how to break abusive patterns in attitudes and relationships that have followed you into adulthood by using your own voice as your guide in a simple, insightful question-and-answer process called the InnerSelf Dialogue.

In practicing this technique, which I've developed and taught throughout many years of individual, couple, family and group therapy, you can learn how to nurture your self-respect, consider your choices on a day-to-day basis and achieve contentment in love, friendship and work. You will learn how use your new understanding to replace the abusive cycle or cycles that have kept you from recognizing and claiming your opportunities and fulfillment.

In the tenth and final chapter, we will discuss what you can expect to encounter as you gain the strength necessary to make—and stick to—positive choices and how you can continue utilizing and benefiting from the InnerSelf Dialogue. We will discuss the impact of a changed you on those you know, who are used to seeing and experiencing you differently. By this time in our journey, you will understand the importance of a determination to use the pain in life that cannot be avoided as an opportunity to grow, develop compassion and experience empathy toward others.

Above all, you will understand how essential it is to avoid the abusive pain in your life. You will find out that much of life's unnecessary pain is related to entrapment in cycles of emotional abuse. You will find yourself beginning to refuse participation in patterns of emotional abuse, no matter how ingrained or familiar they may be. And you will learn how to keep this new ability as an integral and ongoing part of your life.

I know. I've done it. In writing this book, I use examples from my clients and my own life; the healing process and philosophy you will read about is the one I've used and shared with thousands of individuals. I believe in it completely. But perhaps the strongest reason I believe in this path is because it has helped me. In my early years of training, I read case history after case history of individuals who had childhoods like mine. I grew terrified, because in every instance, by age thirty-five they had fallen through the cracks. I was determined that I would be different. You will be too.

1

Parents

To reach maturity, we must separate from our parents.

L ife holds no easy answers and all of us experience the pain and shock of unpredictable events—rejection, cruelty, betrayal, illness, economic hardship, loss of loved ones. What is critical is not the pain itself, but our reaction to it. We all know people who have accepted personal and professional loss with dignity and strength—and those who have not.

Our ways of reacting to life's difficulties are directly related to our family of origin and how we balanced our parents' needs and expectations with our own yearnings for love and acceptance. Children learn the most not from what their parents say, but from what they do: how they absorb success as well as disappointment and loss, how their parents treat them, how they treat each other and how they treat themselves.

All of us grow up in homes created by our parents. Each child enters the family at a different time in the parents' personal and family life, but every child seeks love, approval and a sense of safety in the family home. Not everyone knows how to be a parent. Most parents do the very best they can, but mothers and fathers who themselves haven't been loved well as children may not know how to love their own children. Parents usually believe that they offer only love. But most parents also, often without realizing it, have strong personal expectations of their children, expectations that may have more to do with their own frustrations and their needs for self-esteem and self-expression than their children's welfare.

Children are naturally resilient and learn to balance their own strong needs with the emotional capacities and expectations their parents have of them. Some children accept their parents' expectations and others rebel. But every child reacts to the pressures and conflicts that he or she experiences in family life by developing individual patterns of attitude and behavior. In developing these patterns—even those that are negative and disruptive—children cope with the conflict between their own desires, their parents' expectations and their feelings about those expectations. As this complicated process proceeds, children claim their unique places in their families.

For each of us to reach maturity, three things must happen. We must separate from our parents and learn to stand on our own. We must learn to cope with the complexity and challenges of the world without our parents to cushion us. We also, if we are to be fulfilled and happy, must decide which, if any, of our families' expectations and goals for us are the right ones and when we should formulate our own.

In almost all cases, children who are unable to successfully undertake this process have endured some form of emotional abuse. For as I have said: When emotional abuse begins in childhood, it leaves us vulnerable, entrapping us in negative future relationships with friends, lovers and co-workers and forming an ever-expanding cycle of recurring emotional abuse.

The Legacy of Parental Expectations: Clara's Story

Clara's parents came to this country from Sicily when her mother was pregnant with her. An exceptionally talented seamstress, Clara's mother quickly built up a strong clientele of affluent women for whom she altered and designed highly sophisticated and elegant clothing. Clara's father went to night school and then completed the equivalent of a high school education, followed by intensive accounting course work. Though he never was as successful as many of his "American born" colleagues, his professional life was stable, his personal life fulfilling.

When Clara was seven years old her mother was diagnosed with breast cancer.

The chemotherapy and radiation were long and difficult and during this time her mother could only be involved with her daughter at a minimal level. A talented young artist and a highly sensitive child, Clara missed her mother's companionship immeasurably, especially their days talking, singing, reading and sewing together. Her father gave her what he could, but he suffered from depression during her mother's illness and was not a man to seek professional help.

Clara's mother recovered and once that occurred, Clara became determined to please her. Clara thought that if she did, she could keep her mother alive, well and with her and her father. When Clara's mother recovered, her father's depression ceased and the family united in its former amicable and joyous way.

There was one important difference, however. Clara now submerged who she really was, what her feelings and needs were, who she wanted to be. She believed that it was her job to keep her parents healthy and she spent inordinate energy trying to read their minds in order to please them.

Because Clara's parents were afraid that further pregnancies would cause Clara's mother another bout of cancer, Clara remained an only child. Already their focus, she became the star who brought them light and hope for their own future. Clara's parents expected her to be not only successful but to be *highly* successful, visible and very stable economically. They were so proud that although she was conceived in Sicily, she was born in the United States of America. Again and again they told Clara that due to her birth in the United States, being the first female President was a possibility. They mandated that she go to law school. Of course, she followed their advice/orders.

Clara excelled in law school and began a career in corporate law that made her parents very proud. She was seen as a community leader and achiever. Her husband, whom she had met in law school, was equally successful. They had three lovely children and to the outside world their life was picture perfect.

There was just one problem. Clara hated being a lawyer. Having inherited her mother's artistic abilities, she longed for a professional life where her talent could be expressed. But Clara did not know how to tell this to her parents. The child within, terrified that not pleasing and living for them might cause her mother's cancer and her father's depression to return, would not allow her to become the woman she longed to be.

Finally, when her anxiety attacks became too much bear and at the urging of her husband, Clara consulted me. "We've just moved into our dream house and I keep hearing a voice telling me to get out," was her first sentence. As our work progressed, Clara learned that although she was living the life her parents had dreamed for her, the life was a nightmare for Clara.

Clara's parents, loving people, were heartsick when they learned of their daughter's unhappiness. In therapy Clara learned the reasons for her covering over her adult needs—her devotion to her parents and her fear of disappointing them by claiming her own life—she took a risk and talked to them, explaining everything. To her surprise, they were deeply supportive of the work that she had to do in order to decide how she wanted to live her life. They wanted her to come out of her prison—one created out of a deep need to please. They wanted her to be free.

Clara realized that her expensive new house would never feel like a home and made changes in her lifestyle and career that brought fulfillment and satisfaction. Now a talented and sought after interior designer, Clara earns one third of the money that she used to earn. However, her life is her own. She is using the artistic abilities inherited from her mother, which brings her much joy. Her life feels rich and wonderful in every possible way.

The first step toward a successful and fulfilling life is to understand that we, not our parents, are in charge of our lives and that we have the power to change. We have the power to be whoever it is we want to be and to live however we want. Our lives are our own. Clara was fortunate. Both her husband and her parents supported her growth. After she came to terms with the unintended hurt she endured growing up and discovered its impact on her, she could move forward. Not everyone receives this quality of family support.

As children learn to balance their own needs with the emotional needs of their parents, they do so under the auspices of an often highly charged imbalance. Parents tower naturally over children in terms of their physical size, life experience and skills. Add to that a parent (or parents) who believes that intimidation is his or her right, who wants to own a child as he or she owns a house or an automobile or who can callously disregard and disrespect the adoring eyes fastened upon them, then a dynamic is created which transforms nature's imbalance of power into emotional abuse.

As we think about our childhoods, we may find that because of deep shame and hurt and in order to protect ourselves or those we love, many of our memories are clouded over and indistinct. We may not really be able to say for sure what happened. Also, because emotional abuse so often occurs in childhood, we may not yet have developed the cognitive capacities necessary for long-term memory. Because emotional abuse is often practiced in private, children who were its victims may have been too afraid to retain certain critical information or discounted some experiences and their emotional import because they were told either explicitly or implicitly to do so.

However, there is one element that never fails us in our psychological excavation of our childhoods and that is the present. The way we act now, the way we talk, the way we think, everything from our attitudes (where we stand emotionally) to our postures (the way we physically stand) can be dictated by emotional abuse suffered in our childhood—not only at the hands of our parents, but also by siblings, religious leaders or teachers, in fact, anyone who has had an imbalance of power to abuse and has done so.

The Emotional Abuse Inventory

What follows is a thirty question "Emotional Abuse Inventory" for you to fill out in a quiet, private place. As you think about the questions, try to do so with your whole being. It may be useful to say your own name at the beginning of the exercise, as if you were called upon to be honest before a court. This may help you to transcend the answers that you *wish* were true and focus on the way things really are for you. Another technique is to read the statements aloud before responding. I know this seems like a bit much, but I promise it works. Listen to the sound of your voice as you read certain words. Pay attention to your heartbeat: is it faster? Do you suddenly feel hot or cold? Do you experience any trembling? Sudden physical changes are a signal from your inner voice of truth. Remember, this journey won't be completely pleasant, but it does have a specific goal—the improvement of your emotional health and well-being—and it is a journey that does not permit a short cut.

The statements for the Emotional Abuse Inventory are phrased in such a way that they describe behaviors to which you may be prone some of the time, all of the time or none of the time. Each one is an "I" statement and you merely record the relative frequency of truth in that statement by answering "frequently," "sometimes" or "never." Pay attention to the questions where your ears prick up, to what resonates with you and, above all, be honest with yourself (your honest response is a gift from you to you). Remember: you don't have to show your responses to anyone!

Emotional Abuse Inventory

	Frequently	Sometimes	Never
I am self-centered, even when I don't want to be.	☐	☐	☐
I never think of myself.	☐	☐	☐
I put myself in harm's way.	☐	☐	☐
I ask others to speak up for me.	☐	☐	☐
I am unavailable to my other family members.	☐	☐	☐
I can treat my friends carelessly.	☐	☐	☐
I let my friends take advantage of me constantly.	☐	☐	☐
I treat money like tap water.	☐	☐	☐
I participate in meaningless activities.	☐	☐	☐
I sulk, have quiet temper tantrums or moodiness.	☐	☐	☐
I have irrational outbursts and attack others.	☐	☐	☐
I make self-defeating choices in love, friendship and work.	☐	☐	☐
I am unable to say *No* to the wrong opportunities.	☐	☐	☐
I am unable to say *Yes* to the right opportunities.	☐	☐	☐

Emotional Abuse Inventory (cont.)

	Frequently	Sometimes	Never
When I am successful, I feel guilty.	☐	☐	☐
Minor setbacks can look like catastrophes to me.	☐	☐	☐
I can't make decisions.	☐	☐	☐
After making a decision, I always believe I made a mistake.	☐	☐	☐
I try to control as much as I can in my present environment.	☐	☐	☐
I lash out at my partner instead of communicating maturely.	☐	☐	☐
I am somewhat elusive when it comes to intimate relationships.	☐	☐	☐
The idea of commitment terrifies me.	☐	☐	☐
I look for romantic partners who are unavailable.	☐	☐	☐
I become obsessive in pursuit of a partner.	☐	☐	☐
I run like hell when a good opportunity in friendship, love or work comes my way.	☐	☐	☐
I make poor investment choices.	☐	☐	☐
I rebel against authority figures.	☐	☐	☐
I am sexually promiscuous.	☐	☐	☐
My partner has a tendency to be cruel.	☐	☐	☐
I think yelling is normal.	☐	☐	☐

To score this test, give yourself (2) points for every time you answered "frequently," (1) point for every time you answered "sometimes" and (0) points for every time you answered "never." If your score is over 12, my years of clinical experience tell me that chances are very strong that during your childhood you experienced emotional abuse.

The next step in your healing process is to journal (write in a notebook or diary) about every statement to which you answered "frequently." To the resistant mind, which wants to push the abuse down and out of sight, this may seem like wallowing in misfortune. However, I promise that if you learn to listen to your experiences and treat them as your friends, you will come in time to greater peace, compassion and true freedom. As you freewrite (don't censor yourself as you write—let your thoughts flow) about the statements to which you answered "frequently," try to be specific. Think of times, places and examples, allowing one situation or event to lead to another. Once this work begins, you are well on your way toward healing.

The Cycles of Emotional Abuse

There are five distinct cycles of emotional abuse that begin in childhood and persist in patterns of interaction throughout one's life, unless they are understood and changed. They are:

(1) **Rage**. The anger that permeated your home frightened you so badly that it kept you from thinking for yourself, learning to trust your own judgment or creating your own paths, as well as left you ill-equipped to deal with the legitimate emotional reactions of others. The rage of others you experienced filled you with terror and helplessness. Those expressing their tirades did not care about your needs or feelings. The outbursts you endured were not a "cry for help" within a relationship—i.e. "Please stop hurting me. I can't take it anymore." Rather, they were displaced outbursts that the abuser needed

in order to achieve a sense of power, control and domination over others.

(2) **Enmeshment**. In your family everyone needed to be together all of the time. There was no place for a closed door for privacy, for individual thoughts. The family was expected to be one enormous entity with no boundaries separating one from the other. Your joint interests were mandated and implemented with homemade psychological glue. Such was the way your parents felt safe and secure. You acquiesced, not because it felt safe or secure (in truth, it made you feel edgy and anxious!), but because you felt you had no other choice. If those you deeply cared about tried to enter your family circle, they were treated as outsiders until or unless they were willing to become part of your family enmeshment.

(3) **Extreme Overprotection**. Just when you were at an age to express your individuality and seek a measure of independence, you were smothered by extreme parental overprotection. With extreme overprotection, crippling messages are sent: *I must live to satisfy my parents; I am the center of my parents' lives and happiness; Without their worry about me, I won't be safe; Without them to care for me, I won't be able to handle my life.* The result of suffocating individuality and independence in a child is not only the engenderment of a lack of confidence and inappropriate expectations, but frequently feelings of guilt.

(4) **Rejection/Abandonment**. If you voiced an opinion with which your parents did not agree, they withdrew their love for you, leaving you feeling isolated and terrified to think for yourself. Only if you agreed with them completely and saw everything through their eyes, never your own, would love be shown to you. Understandably, you learned to view love and control as one and the same, trusting neither.

(5) **Complete Neglect**. No one was there for you, ever. Your basic needs like food and clothing may have been met, but there was

never a feeling of emotional closeness or any substantive conversations. This cycle is in many ways an extension and extreme case of the rejection/abandonment cycle (#4). Yet, within it there is no semblance of calm or acceptance, however false and fleeting these may be.

In evaluating most closely which cycle of emotional abuse defines your personal experience, it is important to keep your mind open—there are many complexities that come to the surface when doing this kind of work. In some families, only one parent is an emotional abuser or perhaps the abuser is a primary caretaker of the child. In some families, each parent is an abuser, but abuses differently: for example, one parent may have acted out the emotional abuse cycle of rage, while the other was acting out the cycle of rejection/abandonment. And finally, the abuse can be a shifting combination of cycles within one parent. For example, the abuser can be operating from the enmeshment emotional abuse cycle when the child is fulfilling the parent's wishes, but switches to rage when the child does something to displease him or her. As we proceed to analyze some case histories of the different kinds of emotional abuse cycles which occur in childhood, your best guides to the truth of your own experience are your memories and your feelings about how things really were for you.

The Emotional Abuse Cycle of Rage: Sally's Story

Many people harbor legitimate anger and deep fears, often because of disappointment or pain that happened long ago. Even those who are able to forge new lives for themselves as adults often discover that they still carry the rage that made them feel helpless when they were younger. This is especially true if the people who hurt them still hold any power over them or if they have not faced their inner turmoil, worked through it and left it behind.

The test of our emotional wholeness isn't whether we are frightened or angry; the test we each face is how we *handle* our fear and anger. Individuals who feel helpless often act out their anger toward those who are closest to them. If parents ridicule and humiliate their children or punish them harshly for wrongdoing rather than explain their feelings and patiently show them the right way, they teach their children to punish those who displease them rather than to communicate, reach out and show patience toward others. Those who have been abused emotionally or physically as children often repeat this pattern in the way they treat others. The most violent among us often have been treated the most violently as children. Others who struggle with deep anger turn their anger inward and become physically or emotionally ill.

One of my clients, Sally, expressed her anger in this way. Everything in Sally's childhood home looked perfect from the outside. Her parents were attractive, intelligent and successful. However, that perfection was maintained at a cost. In Sally's case, the price she paid was her self-esteem and sense of play as a child who could not perform precise adult mental and physical operations.

When she was a little girl, Sally learned that as hard as she tried, she could never seem to do anything right according to her mother's standards. Pouring a glass of milk and dripping a single drop would be enough to make her mother scold her for being clumsy. She remembers helping her mother vacuum the carpet and being screamed at, because the fringes weren't brushed to her mother's specifications. In Sally's words:

"My father would come home from work to learn from my mother that I had not been 'a good girl'—that I hadn't helped her enough around the house or helped take care of my little brother—and my father would punish me."

Sally remembers that if she ever showed anger toward her parents, they united against her in a torrent of loud, bitter, ugly and humiliating words. They told Sally their anger was her fault and sent the child to her room, until she was ready and willing to apologize for upsetting them and acting disrespectfully.

In Sally's childhood home, all the floors were covered with plastic. When she came home from school each day, she found bedroom slippers just inside the front door of the house to be substituted for her street shoes. Certain chairs were never to be used. Sally knew that she could not invite friends to her home, because they would bring dirt into the house and might disturb the careful arrangement of chairs and cushions.

When Sally was ten years old, she begged her parents to let her have a friend spend the night. There was obvious tension in the home and during the night her friend wet the bed. When Sally's mother discovered this, the guest was still in the home and Sally's mother began ranting and raging, calling the friend a dirty little girl and Sally a thoughtless one. In tears, Sally's guest called her mother to pick her up. Sally was too humiliated to speak. By midday Sally had developed a high fever with episodes of vomiting and diarrhea. She was too ill to go to school for ten days. As was her pattern, illness in her daughter made Sally's mother solicitous and far kinder. So Sally learned in times of stress, when she was shamed, demeaned and humiliated, never to speak up, never to say she would not be spoken to cruelly, never to say how hurtful and abusive cruel words were—never to say anything. She would just keep it all in and become physically ill in myriad ways. This pattern followed her to adulthood.

As an adult, Sally began to understand that her mother's obsessive habits were defenses against the rage the older woman felt toward her husband. Sally's father was also full of rage and her parents collaborated with each other in an ugly game in which Sally was always the loser: No matter how hard Sally tried to please, her mother would start a fight, then blame her and demand that Sally's father punish the little girl. Making Sally a scapegoat became an emotional outlet for both her parents. Not until she was an adult was Sally able to see that she was an innocent bystander who had been caught and wounded in the crossfire between her parents.

Sally married a compulsive, but not unkind man. Yet his insistence that everything be neat and in order, that she never keep him waiting and that dinner be served at a certain time, often became too much to bear. At such times, Sally would get sick—just as she'd learned to do at a young age and just as her mother had done—and her husband would become kinder and more flexible. As Sally and I worked together, her self-esteem grew and she learned to speak up to her husband, who was horrified when he realized how deeply he had hurt her. He was capable of flexibility and showed this to her. Sally meant the world to him. As she grew healthier, Sally finally understood that she deserved respect. When she told her husband how she felt, her husband told her that (unlike her parents) he had no need to manipulate, use or frighten her. Sally's marriage blossomed as she learned to trust that, regardless of the issues she raised, her husband would not desert or attack her when she stood up for herself. For the first time in her life, Sally knew that she was safe.

A manipulative parent who blames others for mistakes or problems and undermines trust and safety in the home may appear to outsiders as kind and loving. Such double messages may be very confusing to children, who will sense that something is very wrong, but who may not understand and may be thinking, *I must be crazy. Why do I feel so uneasy when my mother seems so nice sometimes and says such nice things* (as in Sally's case when she was ill) *and others say she is so wonderful?* Such manipulative parents may destroy the children who cannot escape them.

Each of us is capable of a range of both positive and negative behavior, the ability to love and the power to destroy. The fairy tale of *Little Red Riding Hood* offers a frank discussion of this aspect of human nature: A child leaves the loving home of her parents to visit her kind grandmother, but before she arrives, a wolf has stuffed her grandmother in a closet and put on the grandmother's clothing and bonnet—the wolf is waiting in the grandmother's bed to devour the child. The child's mother, her grandmother and the hunter who rescues her all represent good, strong adults who can be trusted. The wolf disguised as the grandmother wants the child to believe he is good and kind and he tries to win the child's trust. Yet he is a symbol of the adult who cannot love, despite any disguise he may assume, and who can only use and destroy others.

Many people, even those who act violently or cruelly, like Sally's mother, have other parts of their personalities that are receptive to sincerity, friendship and love. When they begin to trust others and themselves, they can change and grow.

The Emotional Abuse Cycle of Enmeshment: Ted's Story

Parents who try to live through their children and control them usually wish their offspring well. However, such control can produce catastrophic results. How often have you heard a parent say something such as, "My daughter is my future" or "I'd just die if my son ever moved far away or didn't marry someone I approved of"? Many people who feel anger toward their parents unconsciously punish themselves, because they feel guilty about their anger. Some sons and daughters feel so guilty and conflicted about leaving their parents in order to claim their own lives that they make self-defeating choices in love, friendship and work. They become hooked on these negative patterns. A feeling of parental ownership blinds the adult children to the positive choices they can make, sabotaging their opportunities for happiness and fulfillment. Even if they seem successful, they are unable to say *No* to the wrong opportunities.

One of my clients was hooked on this self-destructive pattern of behavior. Ted was an only child whose mother made him the center of her life. Again and again she told him, "Without you, my life would have no purpose." Ted had no siblings or cousins. His mother discouraged close friendships, so he never learned the give-and-take of healthy relationships. Ted's mother anticipated his every need: If he needed a book at the library, he knew he wouldn't have to get it himself—his mom would get it for him. One summer morning when Ted was a boy, he and his mother went to Atlantic City to spend the day at the seashore. Exhilarated by the sea air, Ted let go of his mother's hand, skipping ahead of her on the broad boardwalk. Even though his mother could see that Ted was in no danger, she became infuriated. Just then, the two of them became aware of a commotion on the beach. They could see a lifeguard near the shoreline carrying the limp body of a child. "See," Ted's mother warned, "this is what will happen if you let go of me."

It was a lesson Ted did not forget. Predictably, as Ted matured, his mother felt that no woman was good enough for him. For Ted's wedding to Myra, a lovely and gracious fellow law student, his mother wore no make-up or jewelry and dressed in black, as if she were attending a funeral. After the wedding, his mother made no attempt to befriend her new daughter-in-law, refusing the couple's many attempts to reach out to her.

Ted began his marriage without ever having learned how to live with another person. Without realizing it, he expected the impossible. Whenever his wife was unable to read his mind, as his mother had so often done, he exploded. He took it for granted that he would make every decision and any discussion of differences or the need to plan prompted him to throw a temper tantrum. Then, when Myra became sad, he attacked her by ridiculing her or accusing her of being selfish. When she attempted to communicate by discussing her concerns, he accused her of complaining and told her, "The more negative you are, the more unlovable you are"—the exact words his mother had used long ago, when he had tried to communicate his own anger and frustration at being held so tightly.

Soon the couple became deeply divided over whether to start a family; Myra wanted a child and Ted did not. At Myra's insistence, they began therapy. Each knew that, in spite of the grave difficulties between them, they meant a great deal to each other. They determined to make an unbreakable commitment to resolve their conflict, regardless of the effort it would take. In time, Ted realized that although he was intelligent and successful, he had remained a child. In his words, "I didn't want a child, because I didn't want to stop being one, which is something that a son or daughter of mine certainly didn't need."

As Ted decided to grow up, he also decided—understanding for the first time what this meant—that he wanted to be a true partner to his wife and that he was ready to become a father.

Parents who try to control their sons and daughters are usually blind to the harm they inflict. Some actually believe that they own their children, just as they do their home, furniture, books or art. They believe it is their children's task to do as the parents say, for all their lives. "Letting go" is not in the emotional lexicon of these parents: for them, the concept just does not exist. Unlike some other parents who may act out of emptiness or longing, these parents act out of cruelty.

The Emotional Abuse Cycle of Extreme Overprotection:
Nathan's Story

Parents who love and protect excessively wish their children well and only want to protect them from the difficulties, pain or deprivation that they have gone through in their own lives. However, because they care so deeply, they cushion the road too much and give too much time, energy and focus, determined to make things easier, better, finer and more fulfilling for their children. Because of this overprotection, their children may not develop the natural ability to handle the blows and disappointments of life or develop the confidence to make decisions and right their mistakes. They may be unable to handle failure, learn from it, pick themselves up and move on. Instead, they grow to expect parents to make decisions for them and bail them out of troubles. They also bring this expectation to friends, lovers, partners, work colleagues and employers. They may fail chronically and call home to daddy and/or mommy to make everything right again. If parents hesitate, now that the children have grown into adults, they become furious, because they have grown reliant on this sort of excessive assistance. They usually pick partners to whom they are unable or unwilling to commit—because in their heart of hearts they believe: Who could ever do more for me than my mommy or my daddy? In fact, they are right—what partner/spouse in his or her right mind could live with that kind of expectation!

In my client Nathan's case, though enormously successful professionally and financially, he never developed a true empathy for and consideration of other people's needs or feelings. He went through life thinking he must be central in everyone's life.

Nathan's parents were exceptionally bright and relentlessly hardworking. Their world revolved around Nathan, the older of two siblings. The expectation of him was to study, do well and "We will do everything else for you." In all of Nathan's years at home, he never was expected to make his own bed, help his dad rake the lawn, help his mom do anything at all in the kitchen or even take out the trash. Nathan grew into an ill-mannered and selfish person, though exceptionally bright and, like his parents, relentlessly hardworking. In his home life he never really learned to think about anyone but himself. Why would he have to? The entire house revolved around him. Both parents constantly told him they loved him more than anything or anyone in the world. The message he carried into adulthood was that he, in turn, need care only about them and them alone.

Because Nathan was brilliant in his field, he became inordinately successful. However, he grew up in a home where he was never taught that anyone but himself existed. As an employer, he sometimes could give the same kind of praise that his parents gave him. But if things did not go his way, if someone didn't follow his precise directions, his expressions of outrage could be ruthless and brutal.

Never successful in an intimate relationship with a woman, but enormously wealthy, he became a consummate playboy. In time he married, but he did so only to have children on whom he would lavish the same kind of excessive overprotection and indulgence that his parents lavished on him. While his wife longed for some quiet, private, intimate time, he insisted on constant socializing. Constantly on the run from an inner loneliness he never understood, he secretly envied couples who had a close and intimate devotion, commitment and companionship, but power remained his religion. In time, his wife stayed home to enjoy evenings with their two sons and he began to see other women. Throughout all his successes in life, it was his mother and not his wife who was at his side.

Other examples of excessive overprotection are: All high school and college courses are picked with the parent, rather than giving the son or daughter the message that he or she can do this independently; An important relationship ends and parents arrive at their child's door to coddle, rather than let the son or daughter handle it. This overprotection leaves the adult child open to a relationship with a dictatorial personality who "always knows better." And it can leave even an outgoing young man or woman with underlying feelings of doubt and shame. Again and again I hear from sons and daughters of overprotective parents, "I cannot navigate and negotiate life's slippery slopes and unexpected curbs without somebody holding my hand, helping, assuring me, making it better." Overprotection leads to people who expect too much from their friends, partners who expect too much from their mates and adults who expect too much from their children.

The Emotional Abuse Cycle of Rejection/Abandonment: My Story

My clinical work has taught me that as devastating and inappropriate as unbridled rage is, as crippling as enmeshment can be and as suffocating as extreme overprotection is, withdrawal of love from a child can be even more brutal. Client after client has told me, "At least with anger there is something—even if it is terrifying, but with abandonment there is nothing, no one, no sound, just loneliness and fear." Others have said, " I have friends whose parents just will not let go. They are smotherers who drive their kids crazy, hurt them a lot and get in their way. But guess what! I'm jealous! These parents may be nuts and may be hurtful, but at least they're there!"

I have worked with many clients who suffer from the emotional abuse cycle of rejection/abandonment and their worldview is shaky in the extreme. Sometimes the only thing that can calm them are liquor or pills. When faced with the emotional cruelty of withdrawal, youngsters learn to withdraw themselves, walling themselves off from any intimacy. As adults, they continue to cut themselves off from any fulfilling relationships.

Often they select what is familiar, a partner who punishes and controls through withholding love when expectations are not met and minds are not read.

It is a destructive pattern I once shared.

Much of the energy in my young life was expended in the determination to let no one know what really went on in my family. My friends and my school became my refuge and my rabbi was a source of kindness, support, ethics and culture. Fearing my father's wrath, I drew into myself, keeping constantly on the move so that my terrors had no time to surface. I spoke with no one, ever, about the realities of my home. But because of kindness I experienced from the world outside my home (kindness I trusted because of my experiences as a very young child), I could at least escape my home and find comfort. Many, many children, not experiencing "the village" that cared for and about me during my mother's first illness, do not have my good fortune.

In my high school years, I did everything I could to avoid contact with my father.

Each day, I was the first person to arrive at school and the last to leave.

During my junior year, I began to work at Hutzler's department store in Baltimore two evenings a week. Although I was expected to give my paycheck directly to my mother, I managed to keep some of the money for a college account. My father, knowing that I wanted to attend a women's college, insisted that I apply to a college that required only morning SATs, but did not require that college boards be taken in the afternoon. He believed no such small woman's liberal art college existed. But I found one: Skidmore, in Saratoga Springs, New York. Skidmore accepted my application and the next fall, despite my father's fierce objection and my mother's silent but ever-present sadness, I left home to begin the first period of my own independent life.

During my first month at Skidmore, I did not hear from my parents for two weeks and was unable to reach them by telephone. I dreamed that disaster had befallen them and even that my father had become very ill. When I finally reached my father on the telephone, my worst fears were confirmed: It was a catastrophe, but it was not my father who was ill; it was my mother.

"Your mother is in the hospital," my father told me in a low, angry voice. "If you hadn't left home, your mother's illness never would have happened."

"What should I do? How can I help? Do you want me to come home?" I asked.

My father was silent, always his way. I could picture his angry eyes. I repeated my questions, which were met with impenetrable silence. But I could not back away. I loved my mother too deeply.

The third time I asked whether I should come home, my father said, "Stay where you are—we don't need you here. We never again will."

By my sophomore year at Skidmore, my mother's growing physical and emotional problems were beginning to tear me apart. In my junior year, I *transferred to Goucher College on the outskirts of Baltimore so that I could live at home. Although I commuted to Goucher, I spent as much time as I could on campus, where I developed friendships that meant a great deal to me. My mother's depressive episodes became less frequent. But after my graduation, followed by my move to Washington, D.C. where I began graduate work at Catholic University and met my first husband, my mother's depression worsened.*

Year after year, I did my best to cover up all of the pain I saw and felt, until as an adult it could be covered up no longer.

The Emotional Abuse Cycle of Complete Neglect: Candy's Story

The cycle of complete neglect is an extreme manifestation of the rejection/abandonment cycle. There are no periods of calm or closeness, even tenuous ones, when a child tries to please. Basic physical needs may be met, if economic circumstances allow it. Yet, this is not always the case. Some parents who perpetuate this cycle will use money only for themselves. My college friend, whom I'll call Candy, had such a childhood. There were maids, cooks and a butler in her home. She ate all of her meals with them. Candy's clothing consisted of hand-me-downs from an older cousin. Her parents were out every evening and never showed the slightest interest in anything she said, did, didn't say or didn't do. "To them," Candy told me, "I was and am a nothing, a nobody, a no one." Candy knew that her parents were only involved with each other and that both would remain completely oblivious to her for the rest of their lives.

Predictably, in college my friend looked for love in all the wrong places. And she found it. A minor drinking problem became a severe one. Candy dropped out of college when she became pregnant, giving no one her future address, probably (I now realize), because she did not have one. She did not return to the West Coast, where her parents lived. I called her there twice during my college years. The first time I was told by her mother's social secretary that Candy did not live there any longer and had no forwarding address. The second time I was told to stop calling. To this day, I look for news of my old friend in my college alumni magazines, knowing there won't be any, but hoping that I will be wrong.

Those who have lived a cycle of complete neglect won't need this book to tell them so. But I can tell them that the case histories and healing work they will find, especially those related to the neglect/abandonment cycle, will help them. They can choose to find the strength to believe in themselves and stop gravitating to relationships that confirm the message their parents gave them by their treatment of them—that they were worthless, that they were nothing, that there was something terribly wrong with them.

Though the complete neglect cycle is an extreme manifestation of the rejection/abandonment cycle, I separate the two. It is important to recognize that extremely neglected children exist in all socioeconomic groups. And like all children everywhere who are emotionally abused, they are desperate for care and love.

The Beginnings of Compassion

Compassion for a caretaker, a parent or parents who have instigated one or more of these emotional abuse cycles can be very difficult to achieve, until you are able to realize that they are just continuing a long line of emotional abuse cycles, probably from their own childhoods. If seen from this angle, then *you* get to be the lucky one, *you* get to be the one who learns how to do things differently—and who in turn gets to enjoy the real flowering of intimate relationships with friends, lovers and workplace companions.

Freeing yourself from the emotional abuse cycle already under way comes from understanding that cycle and then feeling the compassion to forgive those who have inflicted harm on you. In that way, you may free yourself. This last part is very important—it is for you.

There are many ways to understand the abuse cycle in which your parents have already been trapped: You can ask them questions or think about the stories from "family lore" in a new way and draw your own conclusions now that you have new insights.

This is what happened to a client of mine, Kate, a homemaker in her forties. Recently, she spoke with me about her strained relationship with her parents.

"Most of all," she began, "I'm haunted by my mother's unhappy life. My father was so cruel to her, but she would never leave him.

"The summer I was fifteen, the three of us took a seven-day car trip to explore the South. But to save money, Dad decided that for five of those days we would sleep in the car. One evening we parked in an old cemetery and it was pouring rain. I had to go to the bathroom and, to be sure no one would see me, I had to wait until it was pitch dark to leave the car. The memory of that graveyard haunts me to this day." The next morning, Kate told her mother that the two of them should refuse to spend another night in the car and should insist upon going to a motel, but her mother replied that her father would never listen.

Throughout her marriage, Kate's mother continued to try to please Kate's father, gradually giving up more and more of herself. "I always begged Mom to leave Dad," Kate told me. "She always said that she couldn't because she had no money of her own—and that was true—but I also think that she just got used to all the misery and couldn't make the choice.

"My mother acted like a child around my father, as though if she could act like a good girl long enough and tried hard enough to please him, eventually he would hear her when she told him he was being unfair. But he never did."

Kate, too, tried to be a good girl—a girl who pleased others, who wasn't allowed to recognize her own needs and feelings and who was never permitted to ask for what she wanted. She became a young woman who was forbidden to express anger, especially not toward her parents. As she retraced the old patterns of her childhood, Kate was able to understand how she had been taught to walk in her mother's footsteps. In time, she was able to reclaim her own feelings, to decide what kind of life she wanted to choose for herself and to set out on her own path.

By seeing the cycle already in place, by acknowledging to yourself the strength and validity of your own insights—which can be very hard to do—you can make a difference in the way you feel about yourself and the way you live your life. To do so may be to take a second, hard look at the others around you who could not break the cycle of emotional abuse and to move on without them. Remember that "survivor's guilt" can be almost as difficult an obstacle to surmount as validating the perceptions of the young person inside of you.

I, too, have felt the pain of survivor's guilt.

As a girl, whenever I was excited about something—a school assignment, a good grade, a new dress, a new date—gloom would envelop my mother. Throughout the wedding ceremony of my first marriage, my mother's face was torn with grief, for reasons that I could not understand at the time. The only thing I did understand was that for my own survival I had to leave her, even though she did not want to let me go.

Now I know that she was afraid to let go of me and that I was very afraid to leave, for just as I had become my mother's lifeline, she also had become mine. We were both terrified of the changes before us.

For many reasons, my first marriage did not succeed and thirteen years later I divorced my husband and gained custody of our two daughters. During this very difficult period, my parents moved to Florida, near where my sister and her husband were living. At the same time, my father continued to control my mother's life.

I wanted to take my daughters to Florida for a weekend visit with my mother, but it was difficult to schedule; my divorce agreement specified that the children would spend part of each weekend with their father, except for once a month. When I phoned my parents to plan my visit, my father told me my mother could not speak to me. Then my sister got on the telephone and told me that the weekend I had selected was not convenient for her or my parents.

"But we're staying at a hotel," I protested. "All we want is an evening when we can take you all to dinner to wish Mother and Dad good luck in their new home."

"It's not convenient."

I pleaded with my sister, but she was adamant. The next day I reached my mother, told her that we were coming to see her and gave her the date. She was silent.

When we arrived, my father and sister were civil but not warm. To me, my mother seemed dazed and frightened, as if she were a victim of mind control. My brother-in-law, always kind, was welcoming, but he was the only one who spoke with us warmly during the brief time we all were together.

That evening, my mother and I were alone for a few moments in the ladies' rest room of the restaurant we went to for dinner. My direct and unplanned words startled both of us.

"You are so smart and so competent," I told her. "For God's sake, get a job or they'll control you forever."

And my mother listened. Soon afterward, she went to work as an office manager for several psychiatrists and she continued to work until cancer devoured her strength. Each working day, she warmly welcomed the patients who received the help that she so desperately needed for herself but never received.

Through the years I continued to see my mother, but it was difficult. I would telephone her at her office to make arrangements, so I wouldn't have to deal directly with my father or sister. When I would arrive at my hotel in Florida, getting together with my family was always a chore. I had little time alone with my mother. During the rare private moments we did have, my mother told me again and again, "I would die without my work." But it wasn't until after her death that I truly let myself understand the depth of her pain. If I had understood it completely when I was young, I never would have been able to leave her to begin my own life. It would have seemed too cruel. In this way, my childhood defense mechanisms protected me until I was strong enough to truly make changes.

Self-awareness offers an escape from the emotional abuse cycles of rage, enmeshment, extreme overprotection, rejection/abandonment and complete neglect. Once you realize and accept what has actually happened in your past life, you can say *No* to perpetuating these patterns, refusing to allow them to keep happening. Remember that one primary challenge of leaving home and becoming an adult is to take back any power that we have given our parents and family—knowingly or unknowingly—that causes us pain. You must believe that you have the right to do this.

Facing life's realities and pursuing positive goals will not happen until we learn to stand alone as adults. This "aloneness" does not mean that we become isolated; it means that we become independent and can form satisfying relationships with others as we navigate our voyage through life. It means we learn to trust our abilities and behave in ways that will serve us well in all aspects of life. With this ability comes the confidence to say *No* when it is best to do so. And then we are able to say *Yes* to the abundance of good things that life has to offer.

It is the feeling of self-worth, of inner dignity, that gives us strength to face terrible pain, loss or fear. This feeling of dignity gives a foundation for our existence, affirming that life is worth living and that despite pain and disappointment, it is still possible to find joy. Once you develop this perspective about your life, you can create a home of your own that provides safety, comfort and contentment. In time, the younger people you affect, whether they be your associates, your students or your very own children, will be able to do the same.

2

Siblings

When there isn't enough mature love in a family,
children are often pitted against one another.

A parent's responsibility is to raise children who develop the ability to love and care for themselves as well as for others. Children who are surrounded by constant sources of conflict or by family members who demean them, play favorites or who cause friction in their lives in other ways, are by definition emotionally abused and regularly develop damaged relationships with their brothers and sisters. More often than not they repeat this pattern in future relationships with friends, lovers, colleagues and life partners.

The sibling relationship represents in many ways our first sharing experience with someone in roughly the same peer group. Siblings usually act toward one another in ways similar to how their parents treat them and each other. However, when there is a significant age difference, there may be fewer opportunities for bonding and the older child may be expected to assist in caretaking responsibilities for the younger child. In such cases, emotional abuse may be more pronounced. In this section of the book we will concentrate on the effect of emotional abuse cycles on sibling associations and their ramifications on brothers' and sisters' future relationships.

How a sibling feels about himself or herself and how he or she feels about another sibling and their pattern of interaction, including their degree of trust, has enormous impact on their future relationships. In a home tormented by emotional abuse, one or more children and an abusive parent or parents may scapegoat the most sensitive child in the family. Another negative pattern is for each child to become a confidant and defender of a particular parent, who is aligned with him or her. In these cases, children are frequently at war with each other about what the "truth" in the family is—about what really happened and which parent is right and which parent is wrong. It is not uncommon for the "scapegoat" and "confidant" patterns to be interwoven.

Sometimes, due to such factors as gender, temperament or birth order, one sibling may bear the brunt of a particular emotional abuse cycle, while another sibling may be involved in a different cycle altogether. Both may become abusers for the same or different reasons. Both may become victims for the same or different reasons. It is very common for siblings who endured similar abuse patterns to gravitate toward friends who have also endured them. It is also common for those who lived with different patterns of emotional abuse to gravitate toward friends who went through similar experiences as their brothers or sisters. An individual abused by a sibling with whom there was always the hope for closeness and love often seeks friends reminiscent of the sibling, hoping in this way to heal through revisiting and rewriting history in a more positive way. Rarely does it happen.

Envy, jealousy and rivalry between siblings are inevitable. With the passage of time, these negative feelings usually subside. Sibling rivalry is an early opportunity to learn that you are not the center of the universe, that other people who have ideas, feelings and needs also exist. The sibling relationship is a life experience that affords us the opportunity to learn to give, to take, to trust a peer and to compromise. However, when there isn't enough mature love in a family, children may be forced to compete with one other in ways that cannot be reconciled, unless they recognize what has happened and work together to make positive changes.

A Checklist for Emotional Abuse Involving Siblings

I have created a checklist that will help you determine whether or not you have been involved in an emotionally abusive relationship with your sibling. Like the Emotional Abuse Inventory in chapter 1, this self-test has a series of "I" statements that you answer either "frequently," "sometimes" or "never."

Before beginning the test, make copies of it and write the name of each of your siblings at the top of each copy. Do not omit a test copy for any sibling, even one with whom you believe you have a stress-free relationship. Go to a quiet, private place and say aloud—yes aloud—(this will make it a more accurate and meaningful test, I promise), "I am now going to take a test to see if I have been or am presently in an emotionally abusive relationship with my brother/sister, _____." Then take the test. Afterward, before scoring each statement, read your answer aloud. Pay attention to your anxiety level as you read. Notice your physical reactions. Is your heart beating quickly? Ask yourself: Do I feel like crying? Do I feel sad? Do I feel bitter? Do I feel angry? Look in the mirror as soon as you complete the test. What do your eyes tell you? What does your facial expression tell you?

Sibling Emotional Abuse Checklist

	Frequently	Sometimes	Never
My sibling teases or makes fun of me.	☐	☐	☐
I am happy when my sibling fails.	☐	☐	☐
I idolize my sibling.	☐	☐	☐
My sibling and I don't see eye-to-eye.	☐	☐	☐
I hide who I really am from my sibling.	☐	☐	☐

Sibling Emotional Abuse Checklist (cont.)

	Frequently	Sometimes	Never
I know which of us my mother likes better.	☐	☐	☐
I know which of us my father likes better.	☐	☐	☐
I know which of us fits my parents' model of the ideal child.	☐	☐	☐
When I criticize my sibling and he or she cannot respond, I feel like I have won a point.	☐	☐	☐
I'm afraid to confide in my sibling.	☐	☐	☐
What I say to my sibling makes its way to my parents.	☐	☐	☐
Discussions with my sibling turn into arguments.	☐	☐	☐

In order to score this test, give yourself (2) points for every time you answered "frequently," (1) point for every time you answered "sometimes" and (0) points for every time you answered "never." Now add up your final score. If your total is more than 6 points, my professional experience indicates that you likely have experienced some degree of emotional abuse in your relationship with your sibling.

Now take all of the questions to which you answered "frequently" and journal about them, slowly allowing your mind to drift back to times and places that you may have forgotten and, in truth, would rather never have happened! As you record your thoughts, let yourself feel what you have written. Let yourself cry. Let yourself get angry and say out loud what comes to mind. Remember, you are in a private place. The walls will not betray your confidence.

After you have finished, read aloud what you have written. You may wonder, "Why does this author keep making such a big thing of reading aloud?" But trust me and the process to which I am introducing you. Remember earlier when we discussed the *voice of truth*, an inner voice that each of us has, but that those who have been raised in emotionally abusive homes have learned to push down and ignore? We are working toward your hearing and trusting that voice.

Ideally, life experience, acquired knowledge and the trust of one's feelings and instincts come together to create a trusted inner voice, which becomes one's truest life guide. With this in mind, as you read, let yourself feel; be sad, be angry and cry if you want. There may be more you want to confide to your journal. Keep writing. Keep reading aloud. Keep remembering and feeling what may have been buried for a very long time, keeping your *voice of truth* buried with it. (Getting in touch with your *voice of truth* is preparing you for the InnerSelf Dialogue Skills about which you have read and will be learning more in chapters 6 and 7.)

Remember, like a ship pulling up anchor, the more flotsam and jetsam that you can find attached to your memories, the more material you can use in healing yourself—and maybe eventually healing your relationship with your sibling.

It is time now to better understand the five cycles of emotional abuse which I have introduced: the cycles of rage, enmeshment, rejection/abandonment, complete neglect and extreme overprotection. It is time to find out how these pertain to sibling relationships which have become abusive. One insightful way is to look at these emotional abuse cycles in other people's lives.

The Emotional Abuse Cycle of Rage in Sibling Relationships: Bill's Story

Bill, a very dear friend who is estranged from his sister, tells me that this estrangement is absolutely necessary, but constantly painful. "It feels," he explains, "like an amputation."

Bill's mother, Eileen, was a young and talented dancer when she married her husband, the driving force in her dance company and ten years her senior. Eileen, though very talented, was not enamored of the dancer's life. She feared what the rigorous and constant stress on the body would do to her; she hated being unable to enjoy a meal without guilt and she longed for marriage and a family. When she married Bill's father, David, she felt that while his interest in and devotion to ballet would remain, he would also be able to be an active husband and a caring father.

He promised this too, but it was not to work out that way. Bill's dad was unable to function as a loving, supportive husband and an available father. Every time his wife or son asked him for something or intruded upon his private world, David lashed out in rage and fury. He viewed his time at home with his family as a time when he should be able to rest and relax and recover from what he called, "the turbulence, demands and injustices of the real world." He demanded a "haven at home" and any intrusion from Eileen and young Bill caused him to fiercely attack his wife and son. He was unaware or did not care that they needed him.

With no support from her husband and having given up her own dancing career that brought her success and fulfillment, Bill's mother stopped taking care of herself. She gained an enormous amount of weight and settled for any crumbs of kindness that her husband decided to give her. "Watching her submission and deterioration as she lived with my father's rage was almost too much to bear. Some days I don't know how I'm still alive," Bill has told me.

When Bill was five, during one of the "crumb" moments of tenderness doled out by Bill's dad toward his wife, she became pregnant with his sister. As unkind and demeaning as David was to Bill and his mother, he expressed the extreme opposite behavior toward his daughter, Martha. Bill's sister, Martha, grew up spoiled and indulged. She was never taught how to show her brother, her mother or anyone in her world respect. She treated every person and experience as if she were the center of the universe. If this center was questioned at any time, she raged and ranted. Her father had taught her well! Her mother feared her and, predictably, Martha treated her mother with contempt and coldness.

However, the lonely, frightened child in Bill never gave up the hope that someday he could trust his sister and their relationship. He continued to hope, even as he kept his distance. Yet he knew that closeness was not safe. For when his sister was nasty and Bill spoke up, he was brutally punished. His father's words and punishment had a sting that would remain with Bill all of his life.

Finally, a few months after his mother committed suicide, Bill sought therapy. His inner demons were such that life had become a nightmare. Bill had given up on the possibility of a relationship with his father years before. However, finally he had come to see that his anger toward his sister and hope for her to change—his impossible hope to rewrite his personal family history—had caused him to gravitate to women as self-centered and cold as his sister. To Bill, his estrangement from his sister felt like a permanent loss. But what he felt as a loss was in reality a relationship that he never really had and only hoped to have. With insight and personal work, his taste in women changed.

He has been happily married for two years.

The Emotional Abuse Cycle of Enmeshment in Sibling Relationships: Lionel's Story

My client, Lionel, is in his mid-forties. Lionel grew up in what he described as: "An unusually close family—we always took family vacations together, even until I was in my late twenties. Friendships with other boys and, later, girls were to be kept to a minimum: My mother was very strict about how long I was on the phone and with whom. And dating was a whole other story…

"But my relationship with my sister, Ellen (six years younger than Lionel), was always supposed to be special. And sometimes it was. But as the years went on I felt like I was constantly breaking her fall: taking care of her in a way that a father would—or a lover even, more than an older brother.

"I lived with Ellen when she graduated from college. She was twenty-one and I was twenty-eight. Neither of us was dating anybody, because in a way we didn't have to, we had each other to talk to, to go with to places like the movies or restaurants. I guess you could say we were dating each other in a way.

"Then I met Karen, who turned out to be my soul mate. We started dating and later wanted to move in together, but both my parents and my sister made me feel guilty and said that I couldn't leave Ellen alone to fend for herself, that I was abandoning her.

"One of the hardest things I have ever had to do was move out."

The cycle Lionel described comes from a family system that is *enmeshed*. Even after Lionel moved out, his problems with his sister were not resolved: When Lionel and Karen saw Ellen (and Rich, the boyfriend she had since acquired) Ellen maneuvered it so that she sat next to Lionel at dinner. Or she called Lionel and Karen's apartment at inappropriate times, like 1:30 A.M., to discuss what the siblings were going to do about some minor family crisis. Ellen's focus, remaining on the nuclear family in which she and Lionel had grown up, became stifling to Lionel. He eventually had to tell Ellen, in as direct terms as he and I could devise, to stop contacting him. Lionel's assertion was calming to Karen, who had begun to dread the kind of sibling situation in which she was smack in the middle.

Over time, as Lionel and I worked together, Lionel and Ellen did manage to evolve a way of talking constructively to one another. It began with a period of no communication at all—a "time out"—between the two siblings. I have found that when I recommend a time out, those from an enmeshed home who have grown to rely on each other too much often learn an appropriate respect for boundaries. When "time out" is recommended in sibling relationships where enmeshment has caused hatred and unkind acting out by one or both siblings, though there are exceptions, they usually do not stop damaging communication and unless each is in therapy, they drift apart. If one sibling loves the other and hopes that things could be different, but they cannot be, he or she then is helped to face the loss, mourn it and move on.

However, Ellen was delighted when Lionel and she resumed contact. The separation helped Lionel to recognize and end a flirtation with his sister of which he was unaware. Ellen was more able, though somewhat grudgingly at first, to respect Lionel's space and his relationship with Karen. Moreover, her relationship with Rich began to grow. Both Ellen and Lionel felt free, truly free, for the first time in their lives.

Because they were siblings, there is always a family of origin bond that Ellen and Lionel will share, but the bulk of their individual realities are in fact separate—and are now kept that way.

Lionel's situation is in many ways the inverse of Bill's, whose story we learned about before. However, while Bill had to accept the harsh truth that he would never have a meaningful bond with his sister, Lionel and Ellen found that through honest communication they could retain and even improve their sibling relationship, a relationship that can be so nurturing and beneficial to human beings. To do so, however, they mutually had to unlearn the enmeshed, negative attitudes with which they were raised and have great patience with each other along the way.

The Emotional Abuse Cycle of Rejection/
Abandonment in Sibling Relationships:
Agnes' and Charles' Stories

Sometimes in emotionally abusive homes, siblings form a healing alliance with each other, a mutual relationship through which they receive love and buffer their pain, as they attempt continuously and heroically to protect each other.

This was the case in both Agnes' family and Charles' family. One of the main reasons why they fell in love so rapidly was that they already felt close to one another. Indeed, they felt as if they had known each other for a very long time. Each had a close relationship with a sibling. Each had parents who tried to control the other by withdrawing all affection if the parents' needs were not met or if one was displeased about a life event. However, in neither home was sibling pitted against sibling by either parent.

Agnes explains her parents' relationship this way: "When my father wanted my mother to do something that she didn't want to do, rather than speak up, my mother stopped talking to my father. My father reacted passively. He wouldn't speak to her either. And so their passive aggressive behavior led to coldness and isolation."

Agnes explains, her eyes filling up as she remembers her childhood home life, "The lifesaver was that my brother and I made a game of it. My brother would be Dad and I would be Mom. At first we just mimicked their behavior and made fun of them. Then we began pretending they were happy together. We would call each other "Dear" and tell each other that we really loved each other and we were lucky to have a terrific family—everything we wished was true."

Charles explains his home life this way: "Mom and Dad had separate bedrooms and mealtime was horrific. The maid served me and my sister, Joyce, while my parents spoke to no one—not to each other and not to either of us." Charles' and Joyce's adaptations to this pain were creative and poignant. Charles explained that Joyce and he had read that parents frequently talk about their day and ask their children about theirs during dinner. So to temper their parents' silence, disinterest and rage, the brother and sister asked each other questions and, in spite of a lump in their throats when they looked at their parents, they continued talking. When young, their conversation was mostly about their daily lives, but as they grew up, they talked about current events. "Then when we could finally leave the table,"

Charles said, "we would go into one of our rooms, giggle and help each other with our homework, knowing that in loving homes that's what parents do."

The abuse, in the form of the rejection/abandonment cycle that both Agnes and Charles felt in their families of origin, affected them deeply. However, because they weren't pitted *against* siblings, when they grew up they were able to fall in love with people who also wanted to find love through stable, companionable and generous marriages.

Their closeness with siblings in this case was of enormous benefit. Later the similarities of their patterns of life brought on an instant compatibility. However, after marriage, all of the submerged anger and pain in regard to their parental relationships began to overwhelm them. To quote Charles, "A tidal wave over which we had no control just began engulfing us." Agnes and Charles were aware of what was happening before their very eyes and against each of their wishes. Nevertheless, all of the comfort they had been able to give each other when they first met evaporated.

Agnes withdrew behind a wall of pain. Charles lashed out at her and then distanced himself entirely. Before long each was reliving the agony of his and her parents' marriage. Still, they were determined to carve out something better for their own union.

Agnes and Charles joined two separate therapy groups in which each could focus on the pent-up, past frustrations they were now taking out on each other and could not control. Moreover, they both worked hard—the pain and resentment bubbled up in each of their therapy groups and could be left there, not dumped on each other. As they spoke about and worked through their pain and repressed rage, they were able to change the cycles of abuse that had become a part of their natural functioning, allowing their love and emotional health to thrive.

Both Agnes and Charles attribute their ability to form closeness to having had siblings they were able to trust. This made them able to commit to marriage in the first place. "If I hadn't had a sister who was there for me when I grew up, there would have been no one," Charles says. In time his parents led completely separate lives. Nevertheless, this sister and brother did all they could, understanding the situation even as youngsters, to support, buffer and communicate with each other. In this way, they saved each other's sanity.

During the nine months of their time-limited group therapy sessions, Agnes and Charles learned that they didn't have to swallow their dissatisfactions, becoming cold and hopeless with fear. They learned to express their feelings to each other as they once had expressed to their siblings. Then the rest was up to them and each resolved to continue to work through their individual problems and develop mature love.

The Emotional Abuse Cycle of Neglect in Sibling Relationships: April's Story

April and her twin sister Catherine did not look like twin sisters and surely did not adhere to the public perception of twins as emotionally close. Catherine had the beauty and elegance of her maternal grandmother, an adored member of the family. Her hair was wavy and blonde, her eyes deep blue. She was long-legged and athletic. And as if this were not blessing enough, Catherine was a gifted pianist and had a beautiful singing voice.

April, on the other hand, was short and wide. Her hair was, in her mother's words, "dirty brown and unruly." April looked exactly like her paternal grandmother, who was hated by both her son and daughter-in-law. April was an awkward, tense and lonely child, so neglected by her parents that her existence was rarely acknowledged by family and friends. It was as if she were invisible.

April and Catherine's father, Robert, had "married up." A talented architect who built "megamansion homes" for the very wealthy, he and his wife were at the social center of their community. April's look-alike grandmother was an immigrant who had been widowed when her son, an only child, was eight years old. She worked tirelessly to support and educate him. During college, however, Robert grew ashamed of his mother's lack of education and social graces and he distanced himself from her. By the time Robert met his future wife, Evelyn, he barely spoke to or saw his mother, a decision Evelyn and her parents strongly supported. Robert and Evelyn were a couple comfortable socializing only in a circle of those they considered beautiful, powerful and important. They took Catherine everywhere with them, while April was left at home.

April always knew her parents hated her. She stopped reaching out to them by the time she was six years old. At meals she was ignored and at bedtime she comforted herself with books and her own thoughts, refusing to let the tears come. But April constantly reached out to her sister, following Catherine around their house and their school like a little lost puppy—begging her for any attention. It was denied.

One day in the school yard, unable to bear April's begging another second, Catherine screamed out for all to hear, "Can't you see that I hate you as much as Mom and Dad do! Get away from me! Just having you near me makes me feel ugly, like you."

The next morning April refused to go to school. She locked herself in her room and refused to meet the school bus. Nobody cared. That morning April took a telephone message for her mother about the time and place of a mother-daughter fashion show and luncheon that Evelyn and Catherine planned to attend the following Saturday.

When Catherine came home from school, April begged her to ask their mother to bring April to the luncheon also. Catherine's response was to quietly and calmly, in an exact rendition of her mother's tone and pitch, tell her sister that in their family she was not wanted—that in fact "you do not exist." April's response was to write down the time and address of the luncheon for her mother and sister, but to write them down incorrectly. The afternoon of the luncheon, unable to contain her rage, shame and pain any longer, April went upstairs to her sister's bedroom, taking scissors with her. She cut Catherine's bedspread to ribbons and then sat silently on the bed, believing that her mother and sister would soon be home. She waited quietly for them, the scissors held tightly in her hand.

However, home was not their destination. Instead, they telephoned Robert at his club and demanded that he meet them for lunch where together they could discuss what happened. After lunch the three went to a movie. While they were there, April took the scissors again, but this time, she slashed her wrists. She later told me about "watching as ribbons of crimson fell on her sister's pink bedspread." When April's family came home and found her unconscious in a pool of blood, they calmly called 911.

It was during April's hospitalization that I met her. While in the hospital under the care of nurses and other medical staff, April blossomed. For the first time in her life, she knew kindness and care. Her parents refused all participation in both family therapy for them and Catherine or involvement in consultations about their daughter's illness and how she could continue to be helped. In fact, they visited the hospital only once, to sign her admission forms and arrange payment for her care. During this contact, they described their daughter as a "genetic mistake," explaining she never really belonged to their family and asked about the possibility of foster care for her, saying they would pay for her care and all of her expenses.

April did not want to go home again. She began to refer to those she met in the hospital as her family. The state agency called advised for April to be separated from her family of origin. Foster parents were found, a devoted, childless couple who had a lot of love, patience and tenderness to give. April has been with them for two years and adoption plans have begun. She has therapy weekly and will continue for many years.

However, April is no longer the same depressed child she was in the care of the parents and sibling who hated her. She has flourished and become what she was intended to be—a beautiful and loved young girl.

The sibling relationships we have seen so far illustrate how diverse such ties can be. Although many times siblings support and care for each other, in other cases, like April's, they can be destructive.

When I visited April in the hospital, reassuring her that things would get better, she asked, "Can you really understand? Your life seems so perfect."

I am the mirror in which my clients see themselves. I rarely self-disclose. I present myself professionally, appropriately dressed, wearing discreet make-up, my hair neatly combed (although showing the wear and tear of the day as the hours pass). Therapists like myself do not intrude on our clients' discoveries by speaking about ourselves. As we listen to them speak about their lives, however, we also think about our own lives. For if we do not have the courage to remember, we will not be able to help others remember. So I remember...

In my own life, my sibling relationship was troubled from the beginning.

My sister and I were not raised to be compassionate friends. I was my mother's child, she my father's. I was the firstborn and I had hated being an only child, especially after my parents moved from the city to the suburbs of Baltimore. I dreamed of having a sister and being her best friend. On my seventh birthday, when my mother told me that I would be getting a brother or sister, the loneliness of my new suburban home seemed to melt away. I remember telling my mother that the news she had given me was the best birthday present in the whole world. I believed that my isolation would soon be over and I would never be lonely again.

When my sister was born, I was thrilled. But my mother was terrified of a dependent infant and deeply shaken by the noise and disruption a baby brought to her well-ordered home. My mother—and later my sister—needed to have a perfectly well-ordered home at all times. To curb her terrifying anxiety, my mother did not allow me to even touch the baby sister I longed to hold.

As the months passed, my sister was not encouraged to be active. I'd sneak into her bedroom to play with her or into the kitchen, where she'd be forced to sit quietly in her high chair. How I cherished my sister! I'd sneak her out of her high chair or carriage and play with her. But then I would be reprimanded by my mother for disrupting her.

On the morning of my eighth birthday, when my sister was five months old, I wrote an anguished letter to my parents saying that because they wouldn't let me hold my baby sister, I was running away from home. Then I went off to school as usual, forgetting all about the letter. When I came home that afternoon, I found my mother and a neighbor sitting at our kitchen table. They were reading my letter and laughing. Ashamed and enraged, I ran outside, where I remained for a long time. By the time I finally returned, I had determined never to speak of the unfairness of my treatment again, to anyone in my family, to anyone at all. And I kept that promise to myself for many years.

As we grew up, my sister became my responsibility. I was her live-in babysitter and anytime I went out, regardless of where or with whom, I was expected to take her, whether I wanted to or not, whether she wanted to go or not. She resented this dictate and so did I. But neither my sister nor I was allowed to express anger toward our parents for their restrictive attitudes and expectations. And so we took it out on each other. I began spending more and more time in school, where I had freedom to express myself, while my sister became closer and closer to my father. My mother simply retreated into herself.

One incident taught me above all others that school was a far safer place than home. One day, when I was about eleven years old, my sister and my father and I were sitting in our den and my sister asked me to move, because she wanted to sit in my chair. I agreed and moved to another chair—but when my sister told me to move again, I resisted, remaining where I was. "You're older. Move!" my father ordered. I obeyed.

A few minutes later my sister told me to move a third time and I refused. "No," I insisted. "I really was here"—but before I could finish my sentence, my father picked me up by my elbows, dragged me across the floor and put me in another chair.

While doing so, he screamed, "You are the oldest. You are supposed to make your sister happy. You have to be the giving one. You know better. I will not tolerate this kind of behavior from a selfish, spoiled brat." Dumbstruck, I remained where my father dragged me for several hours after he and my sister left the room.

Years later, I learned that my paternal grandfather, who had died soon after my first birthday, had treated my father exactly the same way. His preference for his younger son and his disregard for his elder son—my father— pained my father throughout his life.

Yet my father was unable to see how he repeated the pattern.

My response was to bury myself in schoolwork, withdrawing from contact with my father, somehow knowing that my only power was to work hard and escape a home where protection and safety were nonexistent.

The home in which we were raised made it impossible for my sister and me to find any common ground. As we got older, there were several times when I reached out. But she never responded.

On the evening of my father's death, years after my mother's, the telephone rang. I had not heard my sister's voice for a very long time. She was crying. She could not find my father's burial insurance and asked me to arrange his funeral. She wanted to have his body sent from Florida to Baltimore so that he could be buried next to my mother. I assured her that everything would be taken care of. I had only one request—that I be allowed to visit my parents' home for some closure—and to be able to take some personal objects she didn't want, such as photographs of my children, their first shoes, bronzed as a gift to my mother, some photos to be copied, returning the originals to her and a few momentos from my mother for the children.

"Of course," was her response. But after the funeral, when I reminded my sister of my request, her voice took on a tone that sounded to me like our father's as she found excuses not to let me into my parents' home. We have not seen each other since.

There are times, as in my case, when a sad reality is that too much damage has been done to some individuals who suffered cycles of emotional abuse to be able to repair childhood wounds and have positive contact. In such cases when relationships can neither be healed nor buffered, it is necessary to find the courage to end them.

By accepting these realities, no matter how painful, we can recover from the injuries we experienced in childhood, avoid expending energy by dwelling on what might have been but is not, focus instead on what can be and move forward to create a happy and fulfilling life.

There can be a great joy in having a sibling, someone who experienced the same family background as you. Often he or she remembers stories about you that predate anyone else's. A sibling can help you chart and feel grounded in your evolution. If and when relationships between siblings are draining and debilitating, it is always wise to try to work things out and heal them.

When it seems that relationships cannot be healed, one can try to find a way to buffer them. Visits can occur when others are present. Conversations can revolve around safe topics—such as activities, events and films, travel or a beautiful sunset. In this way areas of controversy can be avoided with the hope that the tincture of time and maturity can help make a closer relationship possible.

3

Friendship

We can choose our friends.

"It's just not possible to describe the difference in my life my friends have made," one woman told me. "They've made the hard times bearable and the happy times richer."

There is no joy in life greater to us than the people we love—whether those individuals be from our families of origin or from the families that we create for ourselves. Through our relationships with friends, we can create extended families, not necessarily as a substitute for our families of origin, but simply to augment the living experience. These families we choose will share our times of happiness, give us strength in times of trouble and create memories that forever enrich and inspire our lives.

Our friends who love us truly and deeply—those who touch our lives and those whom we trust so much that we open our hearts to them—give us the strength to believe in ourselves. They give us the power to laugh, to love, to hope and to grow. Telephoning, writing, e-mailing or visiting with friends in person, even once a week, can provide comfort, companionship and perspective.

True friends listen, care and are there for you to share both joy and sorrow. They are not controlling or possessive and they do not insist that you follow unsolicited advice. They realize that each person must find his or her own way; they understand that the right path for them may be unwise for another.

Friendships, however, can bring pain as well as pleasure. Those friends who have proven to be unreliable, possessive, controlling or even abusive probably were treated this way by their parents. Such individuals then later repeat the only pattern of behavior they know with others who are significant in their lives.

Unfortunately, even those who care deeply for us will sometimes let us down. It is important to learn to distinguish between, on the one hand, disappointment, misunderstanding and miscommunication in a friendship, which can be overlooked or discussed and, on the other hand, relationships that, though they may sometimes appear rewarding or even exciting, are primarily disrespectful, exhausting and depleting. Many people are unaware that they are attracted to the latter type of "friendship" choices because of an ingrained cycle (or cycles) of emotional abuse that began in childhood.

Friendships which emanate from earlier cycles of emotional abuse can leave people feeling badly about the energy necessary to maintain the relationship and so wounded and continually hurt that they withdraw into isolation. Withdrawal is a dangerous adaptation. It is important to learn to reach out in positive ways. For the ability to cultivate and maintain positive mutual friendships and develop new ones is essential to our well-being. Without the motivation and ability to reach out to promising relationships, we will miss opportunities to form strong, positive bonds that can enrich our lives as well as change them for the better.

To do this, we must form a clearer conception of what friendship is not. Friendship is not a demand—it is a two-way flow, one based on self-respect and mutual respect. However, many individuals raised in families dominated by one or more abuse cycles do not understand the concept of mutual respect. As a result, many "friendships" involve replicating family cycles of emotional abuse from which individuals within the relationships are unable to free themselves.

Many individuals do not realize that friends can't be made into stopgaps who will fill their voids and relieve the pains that they have experienced. Families in which there are abusive cycles of anger, enmeshment, rejection/abandonment, too much love or none at all, usually produce children who enter the real world as adults unable to cope well, because they feel deep holes in their centers, ones they are constantly trying to fill. No friend can or should be asked to fill this void. It is an impossible and depleting expectation.

With Friends Like These... Who Needs Enemies?

The five main cycles of emotional abuse—rage, enmeshment, extreme overprotection, rejection/abandonment and complete neglect and their overlap—produce a bewildering variety of people in the world seeking friendship through distorted views. Many appear charming, even captivating. I have formed a list, highlighting several types. While you read the descriptions, an example may jump out at you from your own coterie of friends. Just keep it in mind for a bit. Later in this chapter I will talk about how to heal certain types of friendships and how to discern which friendships are in your best interest. These "types" are not just restricted to friendships, of course. You may also meet these people in the blossoming of love relation-ships or in the workplace.

Distorted Types of Friends

- "Swiss cheese" people expect you to give up your self, join their enmeshment and place the fulfillment of *their* feelings and expec-tations before your own needs and priorities.
- "Sponge" people are so demanding—because of rejection, aban-donment, neglect or being "loved too much"—that they leave you feeling limp. They ask so many questions about your life, your

feelings and your activities that every conversation grows more and more exhausting.

- "Crisis" friends—usually a personality resulting from enmeshment—carry expectations from their parents that they become the "stars" who will bring immortality to the family names. These star seekers continuously live on the edge. One achievement brings momentary satisfaction, followed by a compulsive need for another enormous hurdle to conquer. Such "crisis" friends expect you to be on call to help them, to encourage them and to be available to pick up the pieces and rescue them whenever necessary.

- "Ostriches" live in denial about what is going on around them, refuse to understand that they are part of their ongoing poor decisions and expect you to listen with infinite patience about their disappointments in life.

- "Emotional dyslexics" see the world—and events surrounding them—through damaged lenses. Day in and day out they hear and experience things backwards. For instance, a loving man will appear as a jerk and a jerk will be viewed as a hunk. But nothing you say can improve the vision of the impaired lens.

- "Me, too!" folks never listen to your stories longer than it takes them to begin similar stories about themselves. They are so driven by needs to fill emptiness they can only talk about and think about themselves.

- "Bashers" put down everything and everybody. You'll be next.

- "Octopuses" have endless arms, which offer innumerable goodies and comforts in relationships. They entice you with charm and seduction and take over your life, using your strength as their own. Their octopus arms hold you in a prison-like state and you are free only to serve them. In sexual terms, female octopuses can feel like enticing "harpies" who turn into "vampires," while male octopuses are "Don Juans" who become "Draculas."

- "Climbers" have learned to be thieves. They take what they want. These friends relentlessly, but with seeming authenticity and caring, use you, your friendship and those they meet through you to climb. They usually get what they want—this is where their energy is directed—but at enormous costs to their children, who never actually experience true contacts with their parents. Instead they receive the message to be number one, no matter how much others are used or hurt in the process. Furious at their own parents for never giving them true connection, climbers enjoy stirring the pot, doing or saying cruel things, making trouble for others, then smiling sweetly (the "who, me?" attitude) and moving on. I hear the following lament from people used by climbers, "I suffered so much and when I was finally happy, he/she delighted in making trouble for me."

As you mull over these types of friends, you no doubt recognized some people that you know—you may even have seen yourself. It is wise and brave to ask yourself: *What kind of friend am I?* It is always beneficial during this work to strengthen your understanding of your own family of origin—in this case the demands, history and taboos you bring to being a friend. This way, if an important friendship does not work out, you have made the effort to come to terms with your own limitations and background so that you can feel you have done everything within your power to salvage the relationship.

Equally important, you can avoid making a similar mistake in the future. This awareness will cause new ripples of health and awareness in all your valued relationships. As we saw with parents and siblings, there can and do exist relationships where boundaries can be drawn and respect and good intentions flourish. In these positive relationships problems can be discussed and anger understood. In negative relationships there are unconscionable amounts of projection, expectation and destruction. It is important to understand yourself so that you seek positive instead of negative friendships. When you don't, your past history eclipses the potential for happy, fulfilling relationships.

Combined Emotional Abuse Cycles of Rage and Rejection/Abandonment in Friendship: Celeste's Story

In the previous chapters we have looked at examples of those who exemplify one of the five primary emotional abuse cycles in such a way that the features of the particular cycle can be understood. Of course, in real life, things are not always so clear-cut. Celeste's mother was an example of someone who participated in two emotional abuse cycles; on the surface she was all rage—angry, cynical and bitter. She felt she had "married down" and treated her husband as if he were a chair to sit on or a living paycheck. Meanwhile, her ambitions for her children were almost as sky high as her daughter's name: they were to be stars, in fact "celestial." She expected her children to become fiercely ambitious as well as ruthless and taught them her full arsenal of verbally abusive maneuvers to complement their drives. Celeste's mother taught her children that winning was everything and that it was fine to stab people in the back to get what they wanted. She also taught them how to be exceptionally charming. This was easy as they were bright, well-read and cultivated.

If Celeste questioned her mother's tactics or her values, as punishment her mother screamed at her for days on end, labeling Celeste an ungrateful bitch. Then she would retreat to her room, not speaking to Celeste for days—embedding the rejection/abandonment cycle into her daughter's pattern of coping with life—until Celeste apologized for, "being unkind to Mommy, who wants only the best for me."

Celeste's father had a very good heart and, though cowed by his wife's rage, he reached out to Celeste, his favorite child. Celeste remained angry with her mother for what her anger did to everyone in the family, but she was fearful of ever expressing that fact.

In time Celeste married a man who was as ambitious, charming and backstabbing as her mother. Like Celeste, he was raised in a home with constant anger, withdrawal patterns and the demand for success at all costs. Without realizing it, Celeste acted out her anger toward her mother and her husband on her friends, a wonderful circle of interesting people. However, any time one of them revealed pain or difficulty, Celeste took secret delight in ridiculing the person behind his or her back, even as she pretended to be solicitous. If anyone told her she was hurtful, her anger took the ingrained and familiar form of lashing out, followed by passive-aggressive withdrawal.

The healthy parts of Celeste's personality, nurtured by her father's love, acknowledged that her friends expressed upset with her, because they cared about the future of their relationships. But another part of Celeste took great delight in tormenting them— waiting until she felt she had a solid political position—then attacking her friends, sometimes in public. The healthy individuals, the ones with the most self-esteem and no need or desire for emotional abuse in their lives, abandoned this "friendship." One by one Celeste's friends slipped away, until the only ones remaining in Celeste's life were those seduced by her charm and had not yet felt the inevitable sting of an intimate relationship with her. These were acquaintances and professional contacts who depended on her and feared her. All those who remained in Celeste's life grew to expect her inevitable, alternating episodes of outraged screaming and withdrawal.

One man, who works in her law firm, described Celeste's fortieth birthday party as "One of the saddest things I have ever seen: The only people there were her employees and a trickle of angry-looking friends. Toasts by employees were bland and nondescript. Those by friends were just plain mean."

True friends listen, care and are there to share both your sorrow and joy. They are not looking for advantages or for weaknesses that they can later exploit. But some people are so empty, angry or ambitious that they cannot bear to see others enjoy any happiness that they them-selves do not possess. They may be very skillful at hiding this, but when sadness comes to those they envy, their reaction will be insensitive or unkind. In time, other people will begin to realize this and drift away as did Celeste's friends, leaving her in a Dickensian-like fable of what her life could have been, had she realized the ultimate quality in being a friend: the ability to care about someone other than yourself—the ability to love.

However, until and unless Celeste gained a better understanding of how her past cycle of emotional abuse impinged on her adult reactions and choices, this was an ability she would never grasp.

The Emotional Abuse Cycles of Rage and Enmeshment in Friendship: Lori's and Maryanne's Relationship

I noted before that in many cases the cycles of emotional abuse start to interweave and because this is so, things are not as clear-cut as we have presented them in earlier examples. That is often what happens in intimate relationships. One person may be predominantly acting out one emotional abuse cycle, until he or she is faced with a wall—and then an entirely different cycle begins, which may nonetheless be one the person is familiar with, yet has striven to avoid his or her whole life.

When someone abruptly switches the cycle from which they are operating, it can come as quite a shock. Sometimes relationships with victims of the enmeshed cycle of emotional abuse—be they friend-ships, love partnerships or connections to a co-worker or someone in the community—can coast along as if they are truly a gift from heaven until something happens which interferes with the expected closeness and ultimate nature of the bond. At this point the person whom you see and thought you knew is experienced in a totally new way. You may see an angry tiger where a docile lamb existed before. This often hap-pens when a friendship is not a friendship, only a crutch used to deny an abuse cycle that has invisibly crippled an individual. However, as you will learn later, "lashing out" may not be a desire to cripple, hurt or control another. Instead, it may be a cry for help and change when a friend (or a lover or partner) is demanding too much.

Lori and Maryanne had been friends since their teens. Their friendship was in many ways the opposite of a friendship that Celeste could have forged: They had 1,000 secrets that they kept only for the other person. They delighted in their time together and grew closer as the years passed, eventually able to finish each other's sentences. At least once weekly, one would telephone the other and hear, "I was just thinking about you. How did you know?"

But then the "worst" thing possible happened: Maryanne fell in love. Of course, I say that in a tongue-in-cheek way. Her new love, Alexander, was a thoughtful man who treated her with kindness and respect. As the relationship progressed, the times when Lori and Maryanne saw each other naturally dwindled. Sometimes they would double-date, but as Lori was not experiencing the same kind of relationship bliss that Maryanne was, these events became strained and draining.

When Alexander moved into Maryanne's apartment, Lori, without calling to see if visits were convenient, appeared early most Sunday mornings bearing bagels and coffee as she had done for so many years. Since she intruded on the couples' private time, Alexander understandably was not pleased. Maryanne wasn't either, but she felt, in her words, "'Bageled' between two people I really love."

When Alexander proposed, Maryanne was overcome with joy and rushed to tell the first person she thought of, the friend with whom she wanted to share all good news for so many years. But Lori treated Maryanne's news with cold disinterest and an angry refusal to be her maid of honor: "If you think I have the money for that, you're crazy!"

In a therapy session the next day Maryanne confided, "My best friend has broken my heart. This is a happy time for me, but it's also very emotionally intense. Lori won't listen to me for five minutes. It's as if she resents any pleasure coming my way. Her reaction is hurting me so badly that I'm not really happy about my engagement. There's just an awful lump in my throat that won't go away!"

Why was a friend's inappropriate response able to take away Maryanne's joy? Why didn't she realize Lori was acting unfairly and unkindly? Why didn't Maryanne wait for her friend to take time to evaluate her negative reaction and apologize—and if she could not, ask herself if theirs was a "friendship" that could continue?

Both of Maryanne's parents had tormented her with the rage they had carried from their own childhoods and she became the scapegoat for each of them. Maryanne was able to survive, because she was a highly intelligent and gifted writer. She poured her anguish into a journal night after night, week after week, regarding the journal as her closest friend.

Maryanne had always longed for a sister who could become her best friend and confidant, someone to ease her despair as well as her loneliness. She never had a biological sibling but, in her relationships outside the family, Maryanne found a "sister" in her best friend, Lori. They became inseparable and even attended the same college. Each turned to the other in times of trouble, in times of gladness, on days when nothing much was happening, in times of personal or national crisis or just for diversion and to have fun.

Lori, too, endured emotional abuse in her home, but hers was one of enmeshment. An only child, she was overjoyed to have Maryanne as a friend and confidant. However, she was unable to be a generous and compassionate friend because of the anger she felt concerning the enmeshment that she had endured. Down deep, she had the same expectations of her friend that had existed in her original family; she believed that her friend truly had no right to leave her for a happy and committed marriage, relegating her to what she believed to be a "number two" position.

To Maryanne, who had no experience with enmeshment, Lori's demands became more and more bewildering. Nevertheless, what

Maryanne did have experience with was rage and she wanted no part of a friendship that would continue on that basis. Maryanne cared deeply for Lori and, because they had a long and important history, Maryanne worked toward understanding her friend and not lashing out at her because of the hurt and rejection she felt.

Maryanne also began to understand her own unrealistic expectations: due to her lonely childhood she was expecting her friend to "always be there like a devoted sister," which she wasn't and couldn't be. Maryanne's reflection led to the decision not to reject Lori, not to write her out of her life. She chose to attempt to "work out" rather than "act out" and maturely decided to discuss what was going on between them with Lori in order to decide if the relationship could proceed.

As I mentioned previously, once Maryanne had come to terms with the actual way the situation was unfolding, it gave her greater courage to walk away, if necessary, from a long, deep friendship on clear and above-board terms or to continue the friendship, based this time on new and healthier terms—which was eventually what happened.

Lori apologized for her jealous, cold outburst when she learned of Maryanne's wedding plans, describing this "conversation between real friends" as one of the most important in her life. Maryanne used restraint also and she didn't attack Lori for not being the sister of whom she always dreamed. The women's ability to talk together, with sincere emotion and authenticity but no ugliness, deeply enriched their friendship.

Who Are Your Real Friends?

By now, you are familiar with the kind of self-tests that are presented in this book. After you have read the series of "I" statements, respond to the relative frequency of truth in each one with either "frequently," which can feel like all the time, but is really just often; "sometimes," meaning often enough that you have noticed it as a pattern; and "never," meaning, for our purposes, not enough to matter, or practically never.

This test is a little different. Before you do it, I want you to make a list of your friends. On a piece of paper, start with those you would call if there was a bona fide emergency. Then write down the names of those you would invite to a holiday party or to an important celebration. Next, write down the names of those who may be more of your partner's or your sibling's friends, but they still matter to you, etc., etc. After this, make copies of the quiz, putting the name of one friend at the top of each page. Keep an open mind; don't expect the worst or the best; don't expect anything. Remember, we're looking for your inner voice of truth to surface.

One more thing for you to ponder: Those raised in homes where emotionally abusive cycles are ingrained often don't feel good enough about themselves to notice an opportunity to receive caring friendship or to offer it. They often sabotage such relationships when offered. In other words, they suffer from emotional dyslexia. Please view this test as your opportunity to begin to be cured of emotional dyslexia in the friendship department.

Friendship Abuse Quiz

	Frequently	Sometimes	Never
This person doesn't let me talk about my problems.	☐	☐	☐
When I am talking, this person interrupts with a story about herself or himself.	☐	☐	☐
This person lies to me.	☐	☐	☐
This person arrives late for a meeting or cancels our dates at the last minute.	☐	☐	☐
This person criticizes me to others.	☐	☐	☐

Friendship Abuse Quiz (cont.)

	Frequently	Sometimes	Never
This person betrays my secrets.	☐	☐	☐
This person does not accept what I say about how I am feeling.	☐	☐	☐
This person makes cutting remarks about my appearance, feelings, etc.	☐	☐	☐
This person holds grudges for longer than a day.	☐	☐	☐
This person generalizes about my experiences or seems to remember only the bad parts.	☐	☐	☐
I feel that true self-expression on my part will cause this friendship to explode.	☐	☐	☐

Rather than score this test in the traditional way, I invite you instead to consider any friend who scored a "frequently" at least twice. Why would you choose someone like him or her as a friend? What is it about this person that makes you feel you cannot challenge him or her? Or if you have, why would leaving this friendship feel frightening? Upon asking yourself these questions, you may find cycles of emotional abuse in your childhood playing themselves out in the present. You may also find out who your real friends are. Remember: It is the depth of trust and sharing in friendships that bring emotional satisfaction. It is important to devote time and energy to the people for whom the answers to this test were "never"!

Cycles from Our Childhood Are Broken by Choice

My childhood cycles of abuse played havoc with my friendships until I gained insight into the past.

The abuse patterns in the home in which I was raised were a combination of abandonment, rage and enmeshment. I was expected to be there for my mother and compensate for all that my father didn't give her. I knew my mother needed and expected this, as she told me time and time again, especially when I was young, that I was the only person she had to live for, the only person who made her happy.

During my first marriage, I neglected many old friendships, because I had no support in integrating them into my family life. I looked at marriage as an escape from the pain permeating the home in which I was raised, but I brought ingrained reaction patterns—ones typical of those raised in emotionally abusive homes—to my marriage. Though I could speak up and speak out about political and social issues, I was just as afraid to speak up for what I wanted as I had been in my childhood home. The reasons were all rooted in my past. I feared that speaking up would lead to the same abandonment I experienced when my mother became ill. But even more, I feared the wrath of my father who, though charming and outgoing in public, at home alternated between periods of rage and withdrawal if I displeased him in any way or, more accurately, for any reason at all.

As a young bride, I left my graduate program in social work at Catholic University and transferred to the University of Pennsylvania in Philadelphia, where my husband was a law student. Soon after my arrival, I met someone who would change my life dramatically. Yet our meeting almost did not take place.

Elaine was the wife of my husband's former camp counselor. When my husband and I came home to our apartment following our honeymoon, Elaine sent lovely flowers to welcome us. She telephoned several times, inviting us to dinner. But a rule of my first marriage was that I make no social plans without first getting approval from my husband. Accepting Elaine's invitations, it turned out, did not meet with my husband's approval. Time after time, against my better judgment, I acquiesced to my husband. For above all, I wanted the kind of security in my marriage I had never known in my home as a child. And I was determined to do everything in my power to achieve it—at any and every cost.

One day a few months later, I uncharacteristically refused to ignore a voice within and took matters into my own hands. As I left for classes that morning, I smelled smoke in the lobby of our apartment building. When I inquired, I was told that fire had broken out in one of the apartments the evening before. I was stunned and shocked to learn that Elaine's brother-in-law, who lived in the apartment, had died in the fire. I returned to my apartment and told my husband, "I'm going to pay a condolence call tomorrow evening. Let me know if you'd like to join me."

My Baltimore family had observed Judaism in its most traditional expressions and Elaine's was the first Jewish house of mourning I had ever entered where Orthodox law was not observed. Mirrors were not chalked or covered and the women present, although obviously very sad, were stylishly dressed and wore makeup. To this day I well remember the feeling of entering an unfamiliar and foreign world, one where I did not fit in or belong.

Elaine greeted me at the door and her eyes seemed to say that she understood my shock—that it wasn't necessary for me to talk. She took my hand and led me into a quiet room. There we talked or, more accurately, she talked and I listened. Never before had I met anyone with Elaine's presence and compassion. I was completely mesmerized. Although all my closest friends were in other cities, meeting Elaine immediately took away the fear and loneliness I felt in my new home.

From our first meeting, Elaine made sure that I felt Philadelphia was my home. It was in her home that I would meet many of those who would have the strongest impact on my life in Philadelphia and who would become dear and devoted friends to me and my children. Years later, after my divorce, it was through a friendship that began at Elaine's house that I met the person who introduced me to my second husband.

There was rarely a holiday during the time Elaine lived in Philadelphia that I did not hear her voice of sunshine on the phone a few weeks in advance, telling me that if I did not have other plans, I absolutely must join her family for the upcoming holiday. As time passed, our families' lives became deeply and inextricably woven.

Through the years, I marveled at Elaine's joy of living, her love of people and her unique spirit that allowed her to meet everything that life brought to her with optimism, hope, humor and frequent hilarity. Hers was a totally refreshing and unconventional way of living a life. Because Elaine never judged other people, she didn't spend time worrying that she would be judged. She sought out a life that for her would be whole, honest and rich, one that would not hurt others and one for which she made no apology. Elaine sought the path that was right for her and she lived without regret. She sought activity, forward motion and education in a myriad of ways, as well as sincere exchanges and emotional involvement with others. She spoke with me constantly of these pursuits, the ones that brought her joy and eased life's disappointments and pain.

Elaine was always honest, bore no grudges and always lived by hearing and trusting her inner voice. When she loved, she loved deeply and loyally, with no strings attached.

When we understand the impact of our past cycles of emotional abuse on the quality of our own friendships, we can assess if these friendships are ones that should proceed or are relationships that have no meaningful or rewarding future. The goal is to not be intimidated by a friend's anger and moodiness and to avoid friendships where the unspoken contract is: "If you patch up my holes, I'll patch up yours." Or: "I am an empty glass and it's your job to fill me up." Or: "It's your job to compensate for my pain and make my life great." Naturally, there are times when we all feel empty, frightened and lonely. To turn to a friend in these times is appropriate. To be a friend in these times is appropriate. However, if the emptiness or neediness or implied conditionality is a constant presence, it is wise to make changes.

We cannot choose our parents and our siblings, but we can learn to seek out friends who are optimistic, caring and giving. With these friends, we can achieve the art of interdependence. The more autonomy, maturity and self-respect we have, the more able we are to form positive bonds with others who have the independence and the self-respect to give and receive love through friendship.

4

Love Relationships

Falling in love has everything to do with our past.
Love has everything to do with our present and future.

Most people long to fall in love, marry and live happily as well as meaningfully. The art of this accomplishment is the ability to shift from being "in love" to "loving" another, to caring about your partner without selfish expectations or rude impositions. The icing on this cake is to be able to maintain the thrill of being "in love" during precious moments and hours within a loving relationship.

In my parents' day (and, of course, in my grandparents' day), people often married primarily for child rearing, social acceptance and economic security. Love was hoped for, but seen as a bonus. Today we enter marriage expecting intimate companionship and our spouse to be a soul mate. A recent study by the National Marriage Project at Rutgers University, however, has concluded what marriage and family therapists have long known: People long to be married for life, but have expectations so unrealistic that failure is likely.

My life and work have taught me that reasons for these unrealistic expectations are often rooted in the unrecognized patterns of emotional abuse permeating the home and the impact of these cycles on future relationships and marriages. Often we enter marriage or long-term relationships expecting, even demanding, that our chosen soul mate compensate for numerous gaps caused by cycles of emotional abuse, voids which to us are invisible. They are not seen. There are no words to express them.

These voids are created by our extended family experience, by the school and community situations we encounter in childhood. The largest imprint on us, however, is our intimate, nuclear family. Often without realizing or meaning harm, parents and powerful family members pass on patterns of emotional abuse to young and vulnerable members of their families. These messages lingering in our futures make satisfying intimate relationships next to impossible until the impact of the cycles of emotional abuse is understood and broken.

Did family actions (often meant to be protective ones) deplete your self-esteem, make you feel that without parents to care for you and cushion life's blows, you couldn't care for yourself, make decisions, handle difficulties and failures or learn from mistakes?

Did you hear any of the following impairing messages spoken directly or implied?

Emotional Impairment Quiz

	Frequently	Sometimes	Never
I'll make your life effortless, painless and perfect—if you don't leave me.	☐	☐	☐
No one can keep you as safe as I can.	☐	☐	☐
No one can love you as much as I can.	☐	☐	☐
No one will do more for you than I will.	☐	☐	☐
Your primary job in life is to make me happy and give me something to live for.	☐	☐	☐

Emotional Impairment Quiz (cont.)

	Frequently	Sometimes	Never
If you ever care for anyone more than you care for me, my life will be meaningless.	☐	☐	☐
I own you and can treat you any way I please.	☐	☐	☐
You owe me everything.	☐	☐	☐

The journey toward falling in love is rooted in childhood feelings and experiences and in the reaction of a child's loved ones to the child's emerging feelings of sexuality. Such feelings begin when children are very young. Freud used the Greek myths of Oedipus to indicate a son's longing for the mother and Electra to describe the daughter's longing for her father. Both of these situations begin naturally and instinctively. Hopefully, as children grow up they progress beyond this attraction to fulfilling love relationships outside the family. But in cases of emotional abuse, sons and daughters remain trapped and bound to their parental captors, struggling repetitively and reactively against hurtful messages sent, inappropriate expectations imprinted and pain inflicted that they do not understand.

To a large degree, whether or not an individual is able to leave his or her parents and find sustaining love depends on the emotional health within the childhood family.

Those who endured cycles of emotional abuse as children often end up looking for love in all the wrong places with all the wrong people. They ignore opportunities for fulfilling love and sabotage love relationships that could become deeply rich and satisfying.

A Journey Into Adult Sexuality: How a Woman Learns to Love a Man

As children, little girls often fall deeply in love with their fathers and the way each parent responds to her heartfelt expressions will have an enormous effect on how a daughter views herself as a sexual being when she becomes a woman. A girl who senses that her father doesn't love her or that her mother will not share her husband's love with her (neglect and rejection cycles) is impaired, as is the girl who is subjected to her father treating her or her mother with indifference or cruelty or who is privy to her mother's anger about the mother's relationship with the child's father (rage cycle). Also impaired is the daughter who receives a clear message from her mother that she, the mother, must remain the preferred parent or from her father that leaving him for another would break his heart (enmeshment cycle), as is the daughter who becomes dependent upon a father's constant availability to bail her out in times of trouble, making everything much too easy for her (overprotective cycle). All of these daughters will most likely grow into adults whose sexual feelings are tinged with guilt or inhibition—if they allow their sexual feelings to develop at all.

No matter how brilliant and competent she is, a woman adored and protected too much or too constantly by her father will forever remain daddy's little girl, unless she faces and ends this self-destructive cycle. For if a father sends his daughter the message that no future love can be more important than his, she may experience deep fear when she begins to develop feelings of sexuality and attraction toward the opposite sex. She will fail in adult relationships with men, be attracted to a chain of unsuitable lovers and be unable to maintain mature relationships with men and women in friendship as well as work.

A woman rejected by her father may try to cover up the deep hurt of this rejection by avoiding all intimate contacts or by having sex with anyone who asks. She may find it unbearable to be alone and may try to compensate by staying in a state of perpetual motion that leaves no time for rest or reflection. She may become promiscuous, allowing no true intimacy or like Gwendolyn, one of my clients, she may tend to be attracted to men who dislike women.

Gwendolyn consulted me, because she was unable to achieve orgasm in any way during lovemaking with her husband of two years. Prior to her marriage, she could only achieve sexual satisfaction during what she described as "repetitive one-night stands."

The reasons for Gwendolyn's inhibitions and fears became clear in her very first sentence during our first session. She came straight to the point: "I had to wait for my father to die before I could talk about him. Now he can't hurt me any more. And my words can't hurt him. I'm free."

As we talked, I asked Gwendolyn to tell me about her husband and she described a recent incident in a restaurant where she and her husband joined a group of friends for dinner. During the first course, Gwendolyn had an allergic reaction to the salad dressing and began to choke and cough. Her husband didn't seem to notice and continued to talk with one of their dinner companions. However, another dinner companion, the man to Gwendolyn's left, became concerned and insisted that she take the appetizer he had just been served, a warm and comforting food.

My client explained, "His kindness was a complete surprise to me. I didn't know that this sort of kindness existed. Any time my husband notices anything about me, he tells me what I am doing that's wrong. He corrects me in the same rageful, condescending way my father did and then he withdraws all love and affection."

Not having insight into the emotional abuse of her relationship with her father, my client had married a man just like her father. During sex, her body reflected her anger. It refused to open up to her husband, to let go with him, to experience closeness through the language of love: shared trust, caring, intimacy and passion.

A Journey into Adult Sexuality: How a Man Learns to Love a Woman

As little boys suffering enmeshment, rage, complete neglect, abandonment or extreme overprotection, many males learned to fear needing a woman. This fear can make men insensitive or even cruel to the women who love them. This cycle begins when a boy is young and totally dependent on his mother. Girls also resent their dependency on their mothers, but theirs is a dependency on a parent of the same sex so for them there usually are no potentially terrifying sexual connotations as girls grow up. Although many people deny it, early relationships between mothers and their sons include deep sexual feelings. How this delicate relationship is expressed will predict a great deal about a boy's confidence in his manhood and sexuality in his adult years.

The early relationship between father and son is also dramatically important to a son's confidence in attracting and maintaining a love relationship. No matter how much a father and son love each other, they are to some extent rivals. Even the best father feels some resentment at the knowledge that his son may have opportunities that he did not have and that his son will, hopefully, live beyond his own years. If the father is emotionally secure, this reality will not mar the boy's development. However, a father usually treats his son in exactly the same way his father treated him. If his childhood was marred by paternal rage, abandonment/rejection, neglect, enmeshment or overprotection cycles at this crucial developmental time, he will most likely also scar his son's psyche and soul in precisely the same way, with precisely the same means.

About the same time that a boy begins to compete with his father, he usually falls deeply in love with his mother. A close relationship between mother and son marred by emotional abuse can cause the adult man to alternate between affection, aloofness or cruelty. It can lead a man to be terrified of female sexuality and insist that his wife remain in the role of mother or dependent child. A committed wife and mother who is also a sexual adult woman can represent terrifying connotations to a man whose mother has hurt him or refused to let him go.

A mother must not send her son the message that no other woman can ever be more important than she is or that she secretly prefers him to everyone else in the world or that it is his job to give her protection, purpose and happiness. Those mothers who do send this destructive message were probably similarly marred in their own formative years through cycles of emotional abuse.

This is a time when a father must accept that his son's infatuation is just a stage and not something that should make him feel insecure or angry. If the mother acts seductively toward her son at this stage (enmeshment cycle) or if the father feels threatened or angry and reveals these feelings to his son (rage, rejection or complete neglect cycle), the son may develop a terror of intimate relationships.

Once, I was visiting friends when Peter, their six-year-old son, announced, "Daddy, last night I dreamed that you went away on a long trip and never came home."

"What happened to me?" asked the amazed father.

"I don't know," his son replied, "but after you left, I married Mommy and we got along just fine without you."

Fortunately, this father had a sense of humor and he was not alarmed by his son's fantasy. His wife's response was also healthy: She recovered her aplomb and told her son, "Some day you're going to love someone just as much as Daddy loves me and she'll love you, too, and you'll have a wonderful marriage just like ours."

A father who feels threatened by this stage of a son's development or a mother who has not come to an understanding of her own healthy sexuality, but instead clings to her son, implies by actions, words or both that he or she is the most important being in the child's world. This is emotionally abusive, burdening the child with enormous doses of guilt and rage. This stage will be forgotten long before adulthood, but every time the adult son begins to love a woman, his early experience will undermine and perhaps even destroy the relationship. The adult son may also feel uncomfortable in the company of other men and no matter how hard he works to mask this discomfort, trusting other men may be as difficult as achieving emotional and sexual intimacy with women.

The Emotional Abuse Cycle
of Overdemanding and Overprotective Parents

Herb, a forty-two-year old school administrator, consulted me because he'd never been married and felt panicked when his companion of five years, a woman he valued very much and whose company he described as "fantastic," gave him an ultimatum feared by so many men: Marry me, or you lose me!

"My father has made me sick all of my life," he explained, "because he treated my mother so cruelly. My mother clung to me all of my life. She let me know I was all she had. She died of cancer six months ago, but I believe she would be alive today if he had treated her better."

During his teenage years, any time Herb became attracted to a young woman, his mother became physically ill. His father then lashed out at him for hurting his mother, while at the same time the father was rejecting and verbally abusive to her. Herb dropped out of school and secretly saw women of whom he knew his mother would not approve.

"Inexplicably, the more I knew my mother would dislike her, the more I longed for that particular woman. I have always picked women who I knew were wrong for me and they were as abusive to me emotionally as my father was to my mother. At times I couldn't help myself and turned to drugs to ease my pain. I was lucky I was never caught, but I turned to petty crimes such as forging prescriptions to fuel my drug habit, which I finally got under control."

Herb eventually found the strength to receive his high school equivalency degree. He completed evening classes at a local university for both undergraduate and graduate school. Though he did this for himself and cut out drugs and his criminal behavior, he told me, "My taste in women remained deadly."

Herb knew his mother had looked forward to their twice-weekly dinners, when he would take her to lovely restaurants and to the opera or a show. At his present job he met a woman whom he's been with for the last five years. Though they maintain separate apartments, they spend most evenings together. The only two evenings during the week they don't have dinner together were those that Herb had spent with his mother. Now that his mother is dead, Herb spends these two evenings with his father. "I hate visiting him; I feel repulsed when I see him, but feel I must look after him," he explained. "I feel it is my duty."

Herb said, "I guess there are two reasons I'm scared to make a commitment. I'm afraid I'll be a horrible husband like my father was and I can't get over my mother's intense love and need for me. I feel that by marrying a woman, I'm abandoning my mother. I know it's crazy. I know she's dead. But it's as if her longing for me has taken me to the grave with her."

The lives of Gwendolyn and Herb are but two examples of how the delicate sexual dance plays out in every family—how parents treat their children's young and innocent early expressions of intense, enormous love—and the way in which it sets the stage for how the children will feel about their appeal and capacities as future adult partners and lovers.

Exploring Our Sexuality: the Teenage Years

From one generation to the next, sons and daughters grow up in very different worlds than those of their parents. Due to progress in both scientific and social status, they have many more options and opportunities.

In teenage, post-pubescent attractions, some young men and women proceed on their journey toward individuality by choosing to pair up with people who are different from their mothers or fathers. As one such twenty-one-year-old college student explained to me, "There is a lot to be seen and experienced in the world. The world is

my oyster! I'm sick of my parents telling me the qualities and characteristics that I should want in someone I love. Even my grandmother
has gotten into the act and no one shuts her up. I want to round out
my own world and I don't want to be expected to ask permission."

If a parent feels threatened or rejected by a son's or daughter's
choice of a dating partner, one who perhaps has positive qualities but
is not one whom the parent would pick, what can evolve is a hard-
ened cycle in which the son or daughter picks love interests further
and further away from the family's expectations of who is acceptable.
If parents continue to criticize those choices or institute rules
designed to stop this dating behavior, a daughter or son predictably
will go further afield to exercise his or her freedom. This combined
cycle of enmeshment, rage, abandonment and overprotection can
lead to patently unhealthy or destructive relationships.

Because teenagers' relationships with parents and the parents'
reactions to their children's dating or love relationships set the patterns of interaction that influence people's choices of partners for
long-term relationships or even marriage, it is important to understand that pattern in your own life. I want you to take the following
self-test about your own behavior as a teenager. It is again comprised
of a series of "I" statements, where the answer comes in the form of
"frequently," "sometimes" or "never," and you merely respond to the
relative truth of the statement.

Teenage Sexuality Patterns Quiz

	Frequently	Sometimes	Never
I have had sex with partners I did not love or did not even know well.	☐	☐	☐
I pursued people very different from myself.	☐	☐	☐

Teenage Sexuality Patterns Quiz (cont.)

	Frequently	Sometimes	Never
I had to make choices between my family and my dating partners.	☐	☐	☐
My parent or parents disapproved of the people I chose to date.	☐	☐	☐
My parents never spoke positively about those I dated or my love relationships.	☐	☐	☐
My parents never wanted to meet anyone I dated.	☐	☐	☐
My parents expected my dates or love interests to always be part of their world. They never expected us to have time without them.	☐	☐	☐
I had a series of short relationships, lasting perhaps three months or less.	☐	☐	☐
I stayed in a long-term relationship, well after it was clear that it wasn't working for me.	☐	☐	☐
I remained dateless through high school and into college.	☐	☐	☐
I stayed in bad relationships to rebel against my parents.	☐	☐	☐
I left one or more people I cared about to please my parents.	☐	☐	☐
I often think of someone I loved who I left, because my parent(s) disapproved of him or her.	☐	☐	☐

Giving yourself (2) points for every time you answered "fre-quently," (1) point for every time you answered "sometimes" and (0) points for every time you answered "never," add up you final score. If your total was more than 7 points, my professional experience indicates that you have very likely experienced some degree of emotional abuse that led to unsatisfying dating patterns.

Take all of the questions where you answered "frequently" and journal about them—this may be painful, as many of our adolescent memories can be awkward and describe situations where we felt lost. In your journal answer honestly: If the opportunity arose again to be with so-and-so or to have the experience of such-and-such, here's what I'd do now. If possible, try to set up a dialogue with yourself at that age: between the person who didn't know what to do (your teenage self) and the person you are now, a person evolving a differ-ent view of things.

The things to keep in mind are that it is the job of a parent to remain involved, not suffocating, not distant, throughout a child's high school years and that mature conversations on such topics as dat-ing and sex can go a long way towards resolving adolescent difficul-ties and confusion.

If you received no dialogue about these issues or if your choices or expressed opinions were met with rejection, ridicule and guilt/shame messages, there is a very good chance that you are still motivated today by these negative responses or lack of response. You most likely are unaware of them, for they have gone underground into your unconscious. However, they have enormous impact on your confidence, how and with whom you see your opportunities for love and your feelings about commitment.

When the Short-Term Turns Long-Term

As the emotional abuse cycles play out over time, a child who has come through his or her teenage and then college years—who is now an adult in the eyes of the world—may make a premature and incorrect choice of a life partner. Sometimes "harmless" relationships, such as the ones that are merely designed (by our own unconscious!) to broaden horizons or further experiences, are mistaken for real, potentially lasting bonds of healthy love.

In the case of having experienced the emotional abuse cycle of rage, the adult child may feel pushed into cementing a relationship, by way of marriage, to hurt a parent or parents for their controlling, insensitive treatment of them or someone they loved—such as a mother, father or sibling. Often such a marriage can entail an unwise geographical move as well as a foolhardy emotional one.

In the enmeshed cycle, an adult child may make the wrong choice of mate for two very different reasons. First, because the chosen person lies clearly *within* the acceptable range of their demanding parent or, second, because he or she is so far *outside* the field of parental approval. In both scenarios, however, the adult child may end up in a situation where warmth and human comfort are absent or denied. In the emotional abuse cycle of rejection/abandonment or its extreme version, complete neglect, the adult child may marry simply to have someone there, someone who will be in the same room with him or her (even if the partner's listening skills aren't very good) or someone with whom to go places (even if the couple share no interests in common).

In the emotional abuse cycle of overprotection, one who is "loved" too much and cushioned endlessly may be attracted to a dictator-type of personality. Or the adult child may never commit, for after all, who can possibly measure up? Who in the world will ever give as much as an overprotective mom or dad?

Another ramification of the emotional abuse cycles is that the adult child may pick someone just like his or her same or opposite sex parent, because the love interest seems familiar, even if he or she is emotionally abusive. In this way an ongoing cycle of agony continues.

The adult child may pick someone familiar but wrong in a desperate attempt to heal a painful rift with a partner that cannot be healed with a parent.

An individual may become involved with a partner who dominates and intimidates in the same horrid but familiar way a parent did—and feel locked into the relationship as he or she had felt locked into a childhood abuse cycle, continuing to hope with futility to change yet another person who has no desire to be any different. Or, because getting married would express a commitment, two people can live together for a very long time, terrified to marry.

One thing is clear in all of these true life dramas: The adult child is not free to make choices that would benefit him or her, but instead is playing out the reactive patterns dictated by the early, familial cycle (or cycles) of emotional abuse in which he or she still is caught.

Young men and women raised in families tormented by emotional abuse have not learned how to care for themselves (or later their own families) in adult ways. They attempt to avoid facing their feelings of inadequacy or having others discover their shameful secrets.

As a result, instead of becoming whole people, these young men and women become "types." They retreat into certain set ways of doing things that can be roughly classified into four groups which often overlap: the "Warriors," the "Withdrawers," the "Performers" and the "Dictators."

Four Types of Emotionally Abused Couples

Warriors are couples who yell and scream in a constant state of acrimony and ridicule, hurling words and sometimes objects at one another without ever fully understanding the reasons for their conflict. In these marriages, anger is continuous, whether or not it's openly expressed, and meaningful communication is almost nonexistent. As often as these couples let off steam, they never fight hard enough or fair enough to solve their problems together. Though there is physical release through the verbal abuse, there is no understanding of themselves or each other and thus no true intimacy.

Withdrawers are really the other side of the coin of Warriors. Some people learn to express anger by withdrawal: refusing to speak, sometimes leaving the room or the home—or by withdrawal's passive aggressive sisters: joking, ridiculing, teasing and changing the subject about issues they are too frightened and uncomfortable to discuss.

Performers deeply fear the vulnerabilities of love and intimacy with committed partners. Everything in a performer marriage is about appearances. The couple maintain a publicly peaceful co-existence through an unspoken agreement to avoid the intimacy of married love. When both partners are Performers, they keep busy together, sharing projects and experiences, pretending to one another and even to themselves that all is well.

Many Performers choose Hollywood Marriages, completely hypocritical arrangements, in which the players are presented as sophisticated, witty and elegant. Another version of marriage that Performers choose can best be described as Power Marriage. A Power Marriage is first and foremost a business, not to be confused with married partners who are "in love" and "in business," working together on a service or product that allows them to take care of themselves and their family. (More about families in business together is discussed in our next chapter.)

In Power Marriages, a contract exists between two highly competitive people to work together to create opportunities for each other to be successful, reinforcing and promoting each other's goals and ambitions. The partner is valued for what he or she brings to the union, not for the person he or she is. Power Marriages usually start out in a close and invested enmeshment. Each partner believes, "I have met someone who can help me maintain, protect or attain what I must have to make life worth living." Any shared passion is for accomplishment, not intimacy.

Ask them how they feel and Performers will usually change the subject, mimic charming feelings or turn the subject back to you. Because of the cycles of emotional abuse that they experienced as children—they've never been taught to notice or care!—the sad truth is they don't know how they feel. They have been raised to perform for their parents—to fill in their parents' empty spaces and make their lives worthwhile. Performers' *selves* have been imprisoned by at least one cycle of abuse and often a combination. Their dance away from true reality may become so desperate they adopt criminal behavior to cover their inner shame.

Performers often have trouble sleeping until they drop from exhaustion or unless they use pills, drugs, alcohol, promiscuous sex or gambling to ease their pain. By never facing and understanding the true state of their marriages or long-term relationships, they risk damaging their physical and emotional health. They also reduce much of the potential fulfillment and opportunity for creative expression that life has to offer.

Warriors, Withdrawers and Performers can all be **Dictators** at heart. One side of a Dictator's coin is Bully; the other side is Baby. In the Baby mode, there are constant temper tantrums ("I will get my way or else!") and episodes of sulking ("Feel sorry for me!"). Problems are always someone else's fault ("Poor, poor me!"). The Bully dominates through humiliating, badgering, refusing to hear the words and thoughts of another and threatening pain or abandonment. If you are in a relationship with a Dictator, you know it, because for them it's either "my way or the highway." A Dictator is motivated by deep, deep insecurity which manifests itself in the obsession to control others at all costs and to be unconditionally in charge at all times.

A Dictatorial personality isn't always a loud one. Many are quiet Dictators. Some dominate directly, others through manipulation, passive aggressive behavior or a combination. If a son or daughter with this emerging problem is exposed to mature role models outside of the home or if one of their parents is basically kind, he or she may become a Benevolent Dictator.

A **Benevolent Dictator** is a basically kind person who insists upon telling everyone around him or her what to do, how to do it and how to be happy. These Benevolent Dictators usually are not power-hungry, but their insecurities cause them to become tyrannical or to withdraw completely if they feel threatened. Their obsessive need to control arises from a desire to pretend to others—and to themselves—that their insecurities do not exist. Benevolent Dictators who are told that they have hurt someone probably won't understand why and may become defensive, but these dictators usually are able to recognize the pain of others and feel badly for having caused it. From this beginning, a new understanding can evolve. If they choose to see themselves honestly, Benevolent Dictators can change.

The most stifling and dangerous relationship for a child or adult is with a **Malevolent Dictator**. To the outside world, Malevolent Dictators may appear to be models of consideration. At home, these tyrants, motivated by a need for power over everyone and everything, ruthlessly cast out anyone who dares to question them. Like all political dictators, they control through a diet of bread and fear, literally as well as figuratively. Thoroughly vindictive, their expressions of anger know no boundaries. Marriages to Malevolent Dictators are not relationships, but jobs with severe health hazards.

Malevolent Dictators control their partners by doing unkind things, by communicating with confusing messages, by cross examining if questioned and by going on the attack viciously or withdrawing completely if told that their behavior must change. A Malevolent

Dictator who is told that he's being hurtful shows no compassion and will do all he can to destroy the "messenger" in order to avoid seeing himself as others do.

One woman who lives with a Malevolent Dictator told me that everything looks gray to her: "When I do exactly as my husband wishes, when I please him, he can be kind. And his manners are impeccable. He says the appropriate things. He stands when I enter the room, helps me put on my coat and opens the door for me.

"And when I feel so sad and sick because of the life we lead that I can't get up in the morning, he brings me breakfast in bed. He tells our friends about these breakfasts and they say, 'How lucky you are.' And I think, *Yes, so lucky*. But they do not realize, as I do now, that he only treats me well if I obey him or appear weak. If I resist or disobey, he is ruthless and cruel."

Malevolent Dictators can become dangerous if partners ask for change. When change is insisted upon, they may react with physical violence. Because of their feelings of inadequacy and inferiority, malevolent dictators expect their partners to parent, nurture and protect them and they react abusively when their partners do not. In trying to leave these individuals, their partners and loved ones (statistically, abused women and children) are in the most danger of physical assaults.

Women often stay with Malevolent Dictators, because they believe counseling will change their partners. However, the possibility of change through therapy or counseling must be carefully evaluated. Attending counseling or therapy sessions will not help unless an abusive partner becomes deeply and authentically involved in the therapeutic process. Change will not occur unless problems are faced and the abuser stops blaming others and works hard to eliminate all abusive and bullying tactics. However, since many abusers are adept manipulators, it is very important that their partners carefully evaluate the investments the abusers are willing to make in necessary self-examinations, as well as monitor the presence of reliable and consistent changes in behaviors.

Most abused women leave and return several times before permanently separating from their abusive partners. Because of the strong emotional involvement and investment in relationships, separation takes time. Every time women leave they gain more information about available resources and more confidence in themselves and their abilities. Because of the possible dangers in separating from abusers, it is essential women leave in the safest way possible, with knowledge of available resources and a plan for their use.

It's rarely possible, unfortunately, to work through and resolve problems with a Malevolent Dictator. Instead, because what they endure literally makes them sick, their partners often become physically ill. They may live with feelings of nausea, headaches, backaches, body aches and even body sores whose causes cannot be diagnosed. In time, their bodies often succumb to life-threatening illness.

Your becoming or having a partner who is a Warrior, Withdrawer, Performer or a Dictator in marriage means you will never understand your true feelings or needs. This can be tricky to see at first, however, for when both partners maintain their Warrior, Withdrawer, Performer or Dictator accommodations, though much is missing, the marriage may appear stable on the surface.

However, more often one member of the couple longs to stop the performance—the screaming, the withdrawal, the act—and authentically connect to find out what in God's name is really going on. This is something the other partner is usually terrified to let happen.

Therefore, to preserve the marriage, the partner longing for something different pushes his/her inner voice of authenticity down, continuing the façade of a dangerous accommodation that drains and depletes energy, creativity, confidence and feelings of adult sexuality. It is in this state of frustration and longing for something different that the repressed partner often develops an addiction, an eating disorder or another type of chronic physical or psychiatric illness.

But those who seem to enjoy the masks of Warrior, Withdrawer, Performer or Dictator, who use their energy to convince themselves that they are happy and comfortable, are also at risk. Having predictably endured at least one cycle of emotional abuse in their childhoods, these individuals have enormous pent-up anger and sadness. Most likely, they are sitting on an emotional volcano of which they fear losing control and which makes the difficulties and inevitable challenges of day-to-day life almost impossible to bear.

No one can maturely love others or enjoy the world spiritually or sensually under these conditions. People who endure this experience sexual dysfunction, often taking the form of abusive relationships outside of marriage, one-night stands and sexual disinterest at home. They rarely have close friends and live their lives in black-and-white, never experiencing the gorgeous colors of fulfilling human relationships.

The Emotional Abuse Cycle of Rage in Love Relationships: Loretta's Story

The marital relationship is composed of two separate people, but marriage itself is a living entity. Those raised with cycles of emotional abuse do not know how to feed the entity of marriage, thus assuring its life, and this inability puts their marriages in grave jeopardy.

Loretta and most survivors of the cycles of emotional abuse have not learned how anger can be expressed in a way that will work for the individual and his or her relationships.

As we saw with Gwendolyn, experiencing the anger cycle in childhood emotional abuse can lead to an inability to trust, gain pleasure and find release in sexual relationships. Sexual dysfunction typically manifests itself in the inability to achieve sexual intimacy and commitment, the inability to feel sexually satisfied or a need for abuse in order to achieve sexual release. Other manifestations are promiscuity or sexual addiction with no true release or satisfaction.

My client, Loretta, can only release her anger through cruel treatment. Loretta was furious with her parents for the cycles of enmeshment and rage she knew continuously, relentlessly as a child. Once Loretta married Steve, she wanted to avoid intimacy of any sort. Afraid that real intimacy with her husband would unleash a torrent of her suppressed anger toward him and afraid that he would stop loving her if he really knew her, once she was married she avoided him whenever she could. If her husband persisted in his desire to make love to her, she could not become satisfied unless their sex became violent. And, unknown to him, she found a series of other lovers, all brutal misogynists.

After a year of this torment, Loretta came to see me, because she was terrified that her actions would eventually push her husband to leave her. In Loretta's childhood, intimacy and enmeshment were one: Any expression of defiance on Loretta's part was met with her parents' united front of verbal abuse. Understandably and predictably, Loretta's rage about this "prison sentence" made her fear intimacy with a partner. She picked fights with her husband to prevent him from getting close to her and hurting her, as her parents had, as well as to hear and feel his rage which felt like love and passion to her. Yet rather than protecting her, this behavior left her vulnerable to the same kind of loneliness and frustration that she knew as a child.

"The first time Steve and I had sex," she told me, "I asked him to screw me until I almost died. Our sex life was great—until we got married. Now sometimes I just wish he'd fuck the hell out of me every Saturday night and then go away till the next weekend."

Unlike so many women who cherish the time they spend with their lovers immediately after lovemaking, Loretta is repelled by her husband's desire to be close to her after they make love. "I know he loves me," Loretta tells me. "And I love him. But now that we're married, his love keeps me from being turned on. The only men who really excite me are nasty and brutal."

Often those raised in emotionally abusive families have been oblivious to past relationship opportunities with people who were interested in them and wanted very much to treat them well. These individuals grew up in homes where they learned emotional dyslexia so that, as in Loretta's case, the availability of real love makes them want to sabotage it, choosing instead the only way they know—release through torment. We'll see in the next chapter on work situations that those who endured cycles of emotional abuse in their childhood are also often blind to positive work opportunities and colleagues who will treat them well, more naturally gravitating to situations and people who act out in ways that are negative but familiar—deeply ingrained ways they experienced as children. Again, the gravitation is because of the familiarity, but also because of a strong need to make things right.

With this in mind, it is necessary to understand the expression of anger. When one lashes out at a partner with sentences like, "I hate you," "You are driving me crazy," "Stop it," "I can't do this any more for you," "You are asking too much," these outbursts may be cries for help. Frequently these individuals are experiencing patterns of emotional abuse familiar from their childhoods, in which their boundaries are not respected, too much is asked of them and they are being treated insensitively. For them, attempts to change such destructive cycles or behaviors with rational discussion—or even appropriate anger—have been unsuccessful.

Such eruptions, even though they are angry and may appear frightening, should be understood for what they really are—and not experienced as attacks or demeaning, controlling behavior. These are very different expressions of anger, frustration or rage than those of the parent or partner who screams and rants in order to terrify another person into submission and who displays no desire to respect and love family members or bring tranquillity and peace to the home.

If your partner withdraws or is frequently enraged, ask yourself if you are hurting her or him by not respecting boundaries, asking too much, being insensitive. If your partner is angry with you, work to get to the bottom of things. Use sentences like, "How are we missing each other?" "Help me understand what you are asking for that I'm not giving you." However, if a partner is taking out his or her anger for others on you, you can help him or her see this with sentences like, "When you do _____, I feel sad, betrayed, angry, humiliated."

Make it your goal to understand yourself and your partner, not to blame, find fault or "be right." If an argument begins to grow ugly, take responsibility for your own "emotional indigestion" and call for a "time out" until there can be a more rational discussion.

If you cannot make positive changes in your relationship by these measures, get professional help. View getting outside help as a sign of strength, a desire to strengthen your marriage, a gift to yourself and your partner. Through this process you and your partner can give up being Warriors, Withdrawers, Performers and/or Dictators and find real fulfillment together.

Through this process you can develop the ability to achieve satisfying marital relationships based on diplomacy. For the most successful marriages are those of "Diplomats," who realize that finding a balance between "your way" or "my way" and "our way" is a difficult process that takes time, negotiation and an appreciation for a fair and democratic process. When both partners are Diplomats they may often disagree, but they learn how to disagree and make peace by talking and by sharing their problems honestly and intimately. Even if or when their voices rise and things get stormy (which happens in a democracy), both continue to feel safe with each other in a marriage to which they each contribute.

Those who learn to hear and understand their partners with love and compassion—always valuing their partners as separate persons and not as extensions of themselves—achieve the most intimate and fulfilling marriages. They try hard not to demean or ridicule the other's feelings. They agree upon rules for discussion and problem solving. When they're angry or hurt, they go into an agreed-upon private space to work things out. Their anger does not frighten them, because they are safe with each other.

Such democracies are touchstones for respect, authenticity, warmth, love and passion in intimate relationships. More information about how to achieve this is located in chapter 6.

The Emotional Abuse Cycle of Enmeshment and Abandonment in Love Relationships: Dave and Joy's Story

Dave, my client, was a man who kept his wife Joy at a distance, even though he loved her dearly and deeply. Throughout their young marriage, he became distant, moody or critical on a regular basis just after dinner. This was very unsettling to Joy, who always looked forward to their evenings together as close and happy times.

One weekend, Dave and Joy went away for a short vacation they had planned together. The first evening, Dave was very romantic during dinner, kissing her passionately at the table. Later they walked back to their room arm in arm, his wife looking up at him in loving responsiveness. However, as soon as they entered their room, Dave told his wife that he was terribly tired and went to sleep.

The next morning, he wanted to leave immediately. His wife tried to talk with him, to tell him that she felt he was teasing her and leading her on. She was hurt by his rejecting behavior and confusing messages. His response was explosive: He ordered her out of the room, shouting, "Get out of my life, you bitch. Every time I feel close to you, you attack me."

Why did Dave act this way? The story of his early years—and that of his wife's—give insights into their behavior.

When Dave was a boy, his father traveled extensively and usually was away during the week. During these absences, Dave and his mother had dinner together and, after a leisurely, enjoyable meal, his mother invited Dave to share her bed, where they snuggled throughout the night. When his father returned on weekends, his mother gave Dave his dinner early and sent him to bed in his own bedroom, alone, while his parents dined together.

Not until he was an adult did Dave realize how angry he felt toward his father or how his mother had come between him and his father. By creating a situation in which father and son competed for her attention and remained virtual strangers from one another, his mother controlled the household.

Joy was an only child whose parents had died in an accident when she was thirteen. After that, Joy lived in a succession of foster homes. The abandonment cycle she endured was born not from parents who hurt her emotionally, but from the most traumatic life event conceivable in a child's life—the death of both parents. When she and Dave met in college, their attraction was immediate and mutual. Neither envisioned the trouble that lay ahead.

Dave's father, whom he had barely known, had died a few years earlier and Dave's mother was hell-bent against his marriage. Although Dave felt very dependent upon his mother, he married Joy against her wishes. What Dave didn't realize was that his deep dependency upon his mother had filled him with hatred and rage. Dave felt guilty about those nights in his boyhood when he shared his mother's bed and about the unfulfilled desires and sexual tension they stimulated in him. When his wife showed him her sexual attraction to him, she aroused a rage that had been almost completely dormant in him until his lover became his wife.

To Joy, who had suffered the loss of her parents at an early age, rejection was intolerable. When Dave's behavior confused and unsettled her, she would ask him to have discussions he was incapable of holding. Having no awareness of his own confusing messages and behavior, much less the reason for them, he was overwhelmed by Joy's distress. His refusal to talk about the problem reduced Joy to tears, pleading and attempts to hold him even more tightly.

This escalated Dave's rage. He cursed and ridiculed his wife and then withdrew, often for days. This abusive pattern, a reaction to how Dave was treated in formative years—which is what all abusive patterns are—terrified and enraged Joy more. Knowing contact and communication would calm her, she reached out to discuss what happened, causing him to withdraw even further from her.

Until they got professional help, Dave and Joy had retreated into familiar patterns of coping, ones learned as children to cope with life. Dave was a "Performer" married to a woman who longed for an authentic, intimate relationship and was emotionally capable of one. Before her parents' death, Joy's home was loving, affectionate and kind. Differences were shared honestly and, where appropriate, issue-oriented anger was expressed. No one was ever attacked cruelly or personally. However, after her parents' deaths, Joy's loss was so profound that she grew fearful of sharing anything that could threaten her fragile sense of stability. So she learned to "Perform" also, never letting anyone know of her loneliness and despair. In marriage, Dave performed and she tried to also—keeping inside all she felt and all she longed for in order not to rock the fragile relationship that imprisoned their capacities to love each other deeply. Their relationship unraveled until Joy could bear the loneliness no longer and one day screamed a cry for help: "I can't take your teasing or withdrawal any longer. It's therapy or a divorce." Fortunately, deep within both partners was a great love for each other, one neither partner wanted to lose. Dave agreed to therapy.

With patience, time and love, Dave and Joy were able to gain insight into their own lives, to work through and put aside the frustration, resentment and pain in their pasts and to achieve a tenderness for one another even deeper than when they first met.

As you have seen with Joy and Dave, when there is love between couples, if problems begin to be discussed—and appropriate therapy is sought and engaged when love is not enough—change is not only possible, it is probable.

The Emotional Abuse Cycle of Rejection and Abandonment in Love Relationships: Benita's Trauma

A talented writer and published poet, Benita grew up with a rejecting father and an emotionally unavailable mother. Before she reached the age of twenty-one, both of her parents died in a car accident. She married the next year. When Benita first came to see me she was so traumatized that she could not speak. Instead, I asked her to put her problems on paper. This is what she wrote:

"My husband is a very handsome man with classic good looks. He charms everyone. When we first fell in love, my husband told me he loved me so much he'd kill me before he'd let me go. His intensity, his need for me, made me feel safe. I have come to realize, however, that Eric's words have nothing to do with love, everything to do with control and power and that I'm anything but safe.

"When we first started dating, Eric seemed calm, kind, patient and sophisticated. Educated abroad and well traveled, he had a wealth of knowledge that fascinated me. He courted me intensely and I loved what I saw as our compatible interests. But as soon as we married, he stopped sharing his interests with me. He became dictatorial and deceitful, starting with small invasions of privacy. He repeatedly opened my mail and, if I questioned why, he would ask, 'Do you have something to hide?' Always, a terrible argument followed and he would stop talking to me. To keep the peace, I learned to keep quiet.

"Looking back now, it seems my marriage was doomed from the start. My husband had been raised to find a wife who came from a poor family; his mother told him, 'If she has money, you won't be able to control her. If she's poor, you'll be in charge, especially after the children come.'

"At first, I found our arguments impossible to bear. To keep peace, to make things right, I continually said I was wrong and apologized. If I didn't, he would be silent or absent for hours or days. But lately I feel unable to continue this charade. I'm tired of being made to feel crazy every time we have a disagreement. I've begun to stand up to him and in response, Eric attacks me for attempting to change what he calls 'the contract' of our marriage.

"About two weeks ago, my close friend was visiting. As we chatted, Janet said something that stunned me: 'You and your husband are completely incompatible. I think you should leave him.'

"'What are you talking about?' I asked, shocked by her words. Janet and I have never even discussed my husband. I just assumed that she was charmed by him like everyone else I know.

"'I need him,' I said. 'We have six-month-old twin boys. My parents are dead. I'd be lost without him.'

"'And that's just where he wants you,' Janet responded, 'feeling helpless and dependent. You have to toughen up.'

"Then, three days ago, my housekeeper asked to speak with me.

"'I don't know how to tell you this…,' she began.

"'Yes? What is it?'

"'The night you spent in the hospital when the boys were terribly ill…well, something happened here.'

"'What? What happened?'

"'I'm so sorry to be the one to tell you, but your husband had someone here—a woman—in your bed.'

"That night, I confronted Eric. He told me I was crazy and then started packing a bag. He said he's going out of town for a week. He won't tell me where or how to reach him. Since that night I have felt unable to eat or even swallow—that's why I called your office."

The Benefits of Divorce and the Benefits of Marriage

Mention an impending marriage to people and they will likely smile, as at the welcoming of a new baby or a tremendous business success. Mention divorce and they will quietly slink away from you as if you had some kind of communicable disease. Even in today's society, divorce still carries a stigma—it reeks of failure. It is that preconception that keeps people in unhappy marriages and long-term relationships, no matter how hopeless, no matter how emotionally destructive or unsatisfying.

Add the difficulties divorce brings to children, financial pressures and religious convictions and many couples across the globe have resolved to stay together and make it through the best they can. Sometimes the decision to accommodate to a less than fulfilling marriage may be wise. But when emotional abuse is a constant in a home, remaining in that home without hope of change means one is putting one's physical and emotional health in jeopardy. It also means perpetuating the patterns and invisible malignancies of emotional abuse in the future homes of your children. In times of national emergency or crisis, we know that cycles of emotional abuse escalate and that individuals caught in emotionally abusive cycles feel more powerless than ever.

I never want to be in the position of recommending divorce. Ideally, the time to confront the truth of your love relationship is before you take that flower-strewn walk down the aisle. But any time during a marital (or long-term) relationship is a good time to be honest with yourself—to hear your inner voice of truth—regarding the kind of union you have created with a partner and your opportunities for positive growth and changes. With this in mind, I offer you the following self-test.

Take this test in a quiet, private place; read the statements aloud. Pay attention to the reaction of your body. Remember we are working to free your voice of truth, which we will put to very important use in chapters 6 and 7. Respond to these statements as you have the ones before, noting the relative frequency in the truth of the statement that describes your love relationship.

Relationship Voice of Truth Quiz

	Frequently	Sometimes	Never
I can be "me" with my life partner.	☐	☐	☐
I can say "No."	☐	☐	☐
I can say "Yes."	☐	☐	☐
We can disagree, without my feeling desperate.	☐	☐	☐
I am calm and relaxed when bringing up difficult topics.	☐	☐	☐
I can be mildly critical without fear of the retaliation of emotional abuse.	☐	☐	☐
My growth and individuality are important.	☐	☐	☐
We can have fun.	☐	☐	☐
We are intimate and physically close.	☐	☐	☐
I feel enough trust to be able to divulge what is "really going on with me."	☐	☐	☐
My thoughts and ideas are important.	☐	☐	☐
S/he treats me with respect in public.	☐	☐	☐
S/he treats me with respect in private.	☐	☐	☐
The thought of my partner makes me feel content.	☐	☐	☐

Giving yourself (2) points for every time you answered "frequently," (1) point for every time you answered "sometimes" and (0) points for every time you answered "never," add up your final score. If you totaled more than 11 points, congratulations! You are on your way to developing a lasting relationship. If you totaled less than 6 points, however, my professional experience indicates that you might need to consider the origins and future of your present relationship.

Specifically, I invite you to take all of the questions to which you answered "never" and read them aloud again. Journal about them. Read your entries aloud. Remember to pay attention to your body language. Are you flushed? Are you shaking? Is your heart rate faster? Do you feel like crying? Why do you feel this way about your partner? What is preventing you from feeling free and alive? It could be that the issues are primarily your personal problems, not exclusively, but largely. It could also be that you have entered into a relationship based on continuing a cycle of emotional abuse begun when you were a child and not on the firm footings of respect, honor and flexibility. In other words, that you have built your marriage on sand and not on rock.

I have seen couples in marriages built on sand repair the damage of past abusive cycles in their lives, cycles they have unknowingly continued in the here and now—always without realizing the damage they do to all who love them. But this only happens in love and marriage in satisfying ways when both partners work together toward the goal, understanding that marriage is a living entity. If two people don't each contribute to it, the relationship may well turn to contempt and hatred. And the marriage will die.

Honesty with oneself, hearing your voice of truth, is the best way to break cycles of emotional abuse, no matter how deeply they are ingrained. Once the cycles are broken, everything wonderful life has to offer is possible, in one's relationship or with a future love.

5

The Workplace

The hardest part of work isn't the work.

With the subtle threads of power and innuendo, the dynamic in some workplaces may closely mirror cycles of emotional abuse experienced in childhood. The stakes are almost as high: As children we depended on our parents for our literal and metaphoric "bread and bed." In our place of work, we feel dependent on our employer for our livelihood. Think about that word: livelihood—without one we would not be able to care for ourselves or our families. We would not be able to live. Or so we think.

Many of us stay in nonproductive and emotionally abusive work situations long after they have outlived any possible fulfillment or productivity. Why do we do this to ourselves? To a large extent, beyond earning the necessities, the answer lies in the continuity of the emotional abuse cycle or cycles that are familiar to us from childhood days. Each of us holds a place in our family of origin that has an important impact on how we will relate to others as adults, in our personal lives and in the workplace. In order to get along within their families, children learn to emulate their parents' expectations or values to some extent in order to find a role that will help them navigate within the family and get what they want. Also, in order to feel like an individual, each child learns to find a role that is somewhat different from that of other family members.

A boss can frequently correspond to the image of one or both of our parents, either as a dictator or tyrant, skilled in inducing feelings of guilt and worthlessness or viewed as a distant source of approval which can never be reached. In this delicate system of interaction within the workplace, coworkers can become the equivalent of siblings, with all of the attendant problems discussed in chapter 3. Coworkers may become competitive for the boss's approval and attention, working off the model that there is only so much to go around. As a result, you may feel forced to join their rivalries. Coworkers may be lazy, disgruntled and victimized, pulling you into an enmeshed relationship with them. The result, of course, as it was in the family, is that everyone suffers.

I have seen in my years of professional experience that an emotionally abusive working environment is as difficult and painful for clients to understand, accept and act upon as are emotionally abusive parents or partners. To act does not have to mean quitting your job, but sometimes it does. Being honest with yourself about what your real feelings are about your place of employment and whether your employer's or coworkers' expectations of you are reasonable is the first step toward understanding the real dimensions of your work environment.

Stop now and take the following self-test about your feelings about the place you work. The form should be familiar to you now, a series of "I" statements, in which the answer comes in the form of "frequently," "sometimes" or "never." Once again, in taking the test, respond to the relative truth in the statement. Pay attention to messages from your inner self. Be on the lookout for forebodings, sudden movements either in thought or in action—these are the signs we are looking for, your voice of truth telling you what is real despite what may be more comfortable to believe. Remember, clearly analyzing the situation you are in is the first step toward deciding what you can or should do. Keep in mind that no one is going to rush you through this process or decide your truth for you.

Workplace Abuse Quiz

	Frequently	Sometimes	Never
I wish I were doing something else.	☐	☐	☐
When I think about going to work, I feel vaguely sick.	☐	☐	☐
Nothing I do is good enough for my boss.	☐	☐	☐
Nothing I do is good enough to meet my own standards.	☐	☐	☐
I feel sometimes like I am about to get fired, though there is really no reason to feel that way.	☐	☐	☐
My coworkers and I struggle against each other for the boss's approval.	☐	☐	☐
My coworkers and I art not enthusiastic about our work.	☐	☐	☐
At work, there is only one right way to do things.	☐	☐	☐
I fantasize about leaving my job, even though I don't feel I can.	☐	☐	☐
I am disappointed by how my boss responds to my work.	☐	☐	☐
My coworkers and I keep each other from achieving our goals.	☐	☐	☐
I am jealous of other people's working environments.	☐	☐	☐

Workplace Abuse Quiz (cont.)

	Frequently	Sometimes	Never
I am not satisfied by my own achievements.	☐	☐	☐
I feel incompetent.	☐	☐	☐
My boss mistreats me as did my mother.	☐	☐	☐
My boss mistreats me as did my father.	☐	☐	☐

Give yourself (2) points for every time you answered "frequently," (1) point for every time you answered "sometimes" and (0) points for every time you answered "never." Add up your final score. If your total is more than 8 points, my professional experience indicates that you may be experiencing a problem of emotional abuse relating to the workplace.

My message is not that there are always people to "blame" in your present worklife. It's not just this or that set of coworkers or these types of bosses who are causing your problems. You may very well have brought the template for these kinds of problems and laid it over your present reality. This is especially likely if, in seeking to resolve these childhood issues, you find a receptive boss or coworker with whom you can work things out and increase comfort, creativity and productivity with relative ease. But in order to reach the point where you can employ these measures, you must gain more self-knowledge.

This is where your journal comes in. I want you to take all of the statements to which you answered "frequently" and write about why each statement is meaningful for you. Write yourself into a deeper awareness of what you are expecting to happen, who your boss or co-worker might represent to you, what has happened that makes you feel this way and then delve further into what your part in the situation might be. Do this in a quiet place and read aloud to yourself. Let yourself feel the truth of your words. This exercise will go a long way toward helping you discern whether past patterns of childhood emotional abuse are causing your present stress in terms of altering your expectations for harmony and success or whether you really are in an emotionally abusive situation in your workplace.

The Emotional Abuse Cycle of Rage in the Workplace: Paul's Story

Paul is a client in his late thirties. He is the son of an emotionally abusive father. For years Paul endured verbal assaults from his father about his intelligence, his abilities, his looks, his style of dress—anything and everything that might have helped him build self-confidence and success in the workplace. His father had been a factory worker who was promoted to shop steward and eventually to a minor sales position. This did much to alleviate the family's financial pressures, but nothing to give Paul's father a sense of satisfaction about his work. Paul's father hated his job and took every opportunity to let Paul know that if he hadn't been born, the father would never have had to suffer in this way. Paul's father went so far as to say several times he wished he had never had children.

Paul, not surprisingly, became very ambivalent about work as a place of contentment and inspiration. He bounced around from job to job, eventually settling on becoming a part-time director of a cruise ship. Paul cited the seasonal hours, the beautiful locales and the great money as the reasons for his decision, but it was apparent to me that the real reason for his choice was that it was a job furthest from what his father felt forced to endure.

Of course, Paul's choice of employment only angered his father more ("After all of your advantages, this is what you're doing with your life!") and by the time Paul came to see me, he and his father hadn't spoken for several months.

Paul rightly felt that by his age, he should simply not have to bear his father's demeaning and belittling conversation. The negative dynamic of Paul's childhood cycle of emotional abuse was apparent in

Paul's present life. However, as I got to know him better, something else became apparent to me—what Paul really wanted was a job in advertising.

Advertising was a hobby for Paul. He constantly noticed the types of billboards and commercials a company was using; he knew the names of at least a dozen advertising agencies and he frequently composed jingles and slogans for contests that companies offered the public. Once, when he won $500 for "branding" a juvenile book company (i.e., giving it a new name), he arrived at his appointment with me beside himself with joy. I had never seen him as satisfied or optimistic.

Seeing his happiness, I talked to Paul about pursuing a career in the advertising business. The reasons he offered when he rejected that option were all sound ones: He didn't have any experience, he hadn't taken the right courses in college and he didn't know anyone in the industry to open a door for him. The reasons he offered, though logical, were also illusionary. The real reason was fear: Paul was terrified of his father's prophecy that he would fail at any competitive job he attempted.

Time and again I have seen fathers and sons, mothers and sons, mothers and daughters, fathers and daughters and daughters and sons end up working in the same field almost despite themselves. For instance, Paul could easily have excelled at selling the product that his father was engaged in making. The two men had so much more in common than either of them dared to imagine. However, the older man's emotional abuse of his son as a child and into adulthood had made truly getting to know each other next to impossible for them. This made a true assessment of Paul's options impossible for him to see. Unable to know his father, Paul cut himself off from knowing himself and, in so doing, gave himself a classic form of what I call emotional dyslexia.

Eventually, as Paul faced himself honestly, his lens of self-perception began to clear. As a result, Paul found a job as an intern at a respected advertising agency, just a few blocks from his home. He had plenty of time in the off-season from the cruise business to explore this as an alternative and he was fortunate not to be desperate for money (the internship paid next to nothing). Everything was going his way, but then Paul found he faced an enormous hurdle. He had an abusive boss, one who reminded him of his father to such a degree that Paul was cast into the role of ungrateful and uncooperative son.

Paul's new boss, Ted, frequently used expletives when describing Paul's job performance. For instance, if a letter received no response, Ted assumed Paul hadn't checked the address and the letter must have gotten lost in the mail. Ted would then wander the halls cursing him. Once, Ted insisted Paul was arriving late, when in fact he had been on time every day for the previous two months. Paul was frequently subjected to lengthy tirades from his boss about how Paul didn't care about the agency, because he was just a half-hearted intern.

Paul was hesitant to tell me about the problems with which he struggled at work. He felt sure that I, too, would demean him as his father and boss did. Of course, no one ever has the right to speak to another as Paul was spoken to. However, Paul had grown to believe the lies about himself. He had become comfortable both believing them and expecting angry verbal abuse from everyone important to him.

Paul and I talked about self-esteem and about the right to be treated with courtesy and respect. One day Paul spoke up. Ted, his boss, had given Paul a tongue-lashing for speaking directly to one of the agency's clients instead of going through the normal chain of command that the agency followed. Paul maintained that his boss had asked him to make the call and he had only been trying to be "positive and productive," which was the slogan of their firm. Paul further stated that he had told the client nothing that was not common knowledge among everyone involved with the client's work and company.

When Ted continued with his insults and yelling, Paul calmly told his boss that if he could not control himself, Paul would have to leave. It was as if lightning struck! Paul's boss's behavior changed immediately. When Ted saw that he could not push Paul around any further, he reflected on the business side of losing Paul, who was in fact an excellent worker with a dynamic future and who cost the company practically nothing to employ.

Paul's boss did not become a changed man. His natural communication pattern and style was emotionally abusive and clearly marked him as a dictator. (Dictators don't only exist in love relationships, as we read about in the last chapter, but in the boardroom too!) Ted alternated between periods of being a bully and a sulking baby and those patterns probably persist to this day. But with Paul's growing awareness, he was able to speak up for himself—affirm that enough is enough!—and in this way educate Ted about Paul's limits and expectations as an employee.

People who have been intimidated by their parents or other important family members may not know any other ways to communicate. A dictator in the workplace can be very intimidating and can make everyone miserable. Dictators also wreak havoc and do grave damage on for-profit and non-profit boards of directors and in volunteer organizations. A dictator in a leadership role in a community effort will resent other talented members who want to contribute. They will do anything and everything possible to push out those they view as competition. They will conduct business or other activities in such a way that talented, creative individuals who want to contribute will drift away.

I have seen chosen leaders drain their companies of all humanity and decency. I have observed power-hungry individuals heading volunteer and charity organizations who take every opportunity to discourage the talented people they secretly envy for their vision and abilities to work hard, motivate others and achieve goals. In doing so, dictators rob the heart and soul of the organizations they were chosen to lead.

Frequently (but not always), dictators are intelligent and, like other abusive people, they often develop an ability to be charming to mask their abusive behaviors. They usually have enormous bravado and may engage compulsively in highly competitive physical activities to demonstrate their power.

Nevertheless, dictatorial personalities are immature and under their bravado, are very unsure of themselves. Anyone who has lived with or worked with one knows his/her underbelly—a childish whiner who pouts or throws temper tantrums when things don't go well. Anyone who has lived with the bully/baby personality knows it goes hand in hand with picking fights, verbal abuse and the desperate need to control everyone and everything.

People who feel good about themselves don't act this way. Mature people don't want to control or bully anyone and they know that this behavior doesn't produce loyalty or respect. Mature people want to communicate, to lead or be led, to guide or be guided. But dictators in the workplace don't know how to control their aggressive tendencies. The energy and aggression they express through bullying others may be misread as strength, but real strength lies in being able to treat others respectfully.

If you work for a dictator and need to stay in your present job, keep your sense of humor and remember that the bully's behavior toward you isn't personal. Respect yourself and work to your finest ability. Even a bully respects someone who has pride and gives a good day's work and an intelligent bully will choose a target who seems more vulnerable, as Paul's boss was forced to do. In the meantime, Paul developed a circle of supportive friends at work and is getting great advertising experience. He also has begun to work toward an MBA in advertising at night and plans to leave the agency when he gets his degree.

Paul could very easily have turned into a "pot-stirrer," which is how victims of the emotional abuse cycle of rage frequently act out.

As a child, the only way Paul could get positive attention from his father was to report to his dad any time his older brother, Neil, broke a family rule, i.e., lights out by 11:00, no smoking, no curse words (though such words were fine for his father to use!).

Paul also got attention by causing trouble between Neil and their younger sibling, Katie. This "stirring the pot" behavior did occasionally bring the reward of time and attention from his father, although predictably it destroyed Paul's relationships with his brother and sister. In knee jerk reaction, children who don't receive mature parental love and who feel pitted against their brothers or sisters may grow into adults who act out this unfinished business in the workplace, forever viewing their coworkers as rivals in just the same way they viewed their siblings, as they fought as hard as they could for parental love.

Though Paul could easily have brought his ingrained family behavior to his workplace by setting up two colleagues to argue whenever he felt the heat or manipulating in order to achieve "satisfaction" in much the same way he did as a child, he chose a far better path.

He chose to state clearly and with dignity what he wanted and expected and he got it. Then Paul began to chart his own professional course by establishing his goals and developing a plan to achieve them.

Cycles of emotional abuse produce differing "types" of employers and employees. Given the opportunity, many become dictators. For example, you will encounter people who demand more than their fair share of recognition, praise and power—for which others around them in the work environment can pay quite a price. Through ambition, manipulation and being in the right place at the right time, these "star seekers" will rise to the top. Sometimes they are the offspring of parents determined to live through them and grow famous through them. A true star is someone who cares about people, knows how to treat them and who can lead but also follow. This person is very different than a "star seeker," one in desperate need of playing the lead role, not caring how he or she gets there or who is hurt in the process.

You may work with or for a "complainer." Complainers are martyrs determined to get attention by consistent whining. I'm not talking about someone with a difficult problem or burden who asks for help or support. Reaching out in this way is an appropriate and healthy thing to do. No, a complainer is the kind of person who can find anything about which to be miserable. He or she is a perpetual victim who whines constantly and sulks silently—letting you know that this particular misery is especially unbearable, as, of course, have been all the others. There are, of course, myriad other office personalities—backstabbers, sneaks, know-it-alls—all of which are adaptations learned in childhood.

One of the most common problems faced by adult children who endured one or more cycles of emotional abuse growing up is not choosing a job that really motivates them, but having been forced to make future career choices early to please one or both parents. This can manifest as a parental commandment for them to enter a profession or, conversely, to work with their hands; to work with a lot of people or by themselves, in one geographical area or another. Parents who make such demands do so because their children's independence and individuality are too threatening to them. Therefore an unusual choice of employment, which may benefit a son or daughter on his or her own path to individuation, becomes especially alarming.

Examples of inappropriate, pressured job choices are prevalent in today's world, but nowhere do cycles of emotional abuse come so clearly into focus as in family businesses. Some men and women are unhappy at work, because they have felt compelled to join family businesses to please their parents, even though the businesses or professions are not right for them. This can happen when parents don't give their sons and daughters opportunities to know their own minds or to express their feelings about what would be best for them. When adult children are forced into family businesses by parents, competent colleagues will realize this and will resent the son or daughter, adding strain to the workplace.

In family businesses, emotional abuse can be an enormously complicated experience that drains energy from the whole staff. In businesses where parents have trouble giving up control, their sons and daughters will have very hard times working productively and company morale will suffer. Of course, if the family business and the family are ones in which everyone is valued and respected, family members will be able to express differences of opinion without fear. Generally, however, parents who stand in the way of their offsprings' growth don't make requests; they issue orders. Sons and daughters of these parents may feel too frightened and intimidated to disobey their parents' wishes, just as had been the case when they were children. As their inner rage reaches a boiling point, their submission erodes their already fragile self-esteem.

In unhealthy family businesses, adult offspring are often referred to as "children" rather than being called by name and referred to as sons and daughters. These men and women do not feel economically or emotionally self-sufficient. This is a feature present in all emotionally abusive workplaces: The employees are considered and treated as if they were beneath the "bosses," regardless of age, experience or creativity.

It is appropriate to exercise restraint and show respect to the organizational positions above oneself in the hierarchy. But to be afraid to give opinions—fearing that money or opportunities will be taken away from you if you do—is always a characteristic of a poor work environment. It is especially prevalent in family businesses where cycles of emotional abuse prevail. Sometimes in family businesses this is taken to extremes and the employees have the extra strain of fearing that relatives of the boss will "gain" over them.

Siblings who work together and who were not given mature love in their childhood homes may, in adulthood, be brutally vying against each other in the workplace to compete for this love without even realizing it. In these cases, the employees of the company will be forced to choose sides and the anxiety level throughout the company will be high. This situation is even more complicated when cousins and other extended family members also are active in family businesses.

The Emotional Abuse Cycles of Enmeshment, Abandonment and Overprotection in the Workplace: the Johnsons' Story

To most immigrant families, enmeshment is a normal way to live. It assures survival. However, after the first generation dies off, the second generation often begins to bristle at being denied the right to their own individuality. Such was the case in the family of Willie and Tess, each first generation, who had Americanized their original Polish names. It was predominantly the enmeshment cycle, with a sizable dose of rejection, that was at work in the vast used car business built by what Willie described as his "blood, sweat and tears."

Two of Willie's sons and his daughter worked for the company. Priscilla was the youngest and the favorite child. Tess had longed for a daughter and nothing that her sons Bruce and Henry did gave her enough joy to compensate for "only having sons." Her husband really did not want a third child, but acquiesced because of his wife's desperate desire for a daughter.

When Priscilla was born, her mother withdrew from any closeness to her two sons, devoting herself solely to her daughter. "My wish has finally come true—a daughter," she told all who would listen. Always something of a complainer, now her whining consisted of complaints that there never would be time enough for her to give to Priscilla all that the child deserved. From her first moments on earth,

Priscilla became a quintessential example of a child who was overprotected, overindulged and loved much too much for her own good,
as well as the good of the family.

The care and support of Bruce and Henry was taken over by their
father, who did what he could to help and guide them and make up
for their mother's rejection. Willie was also enamored by Priscilla's
femininity and charm and his affection toward her, coupled with his
wife's complete involvement with the girl, frightened and angered
Bruce and Henry. As they grew older, their fear and anger grew with
them.

Bruce learned to get attention at home by furious outbursts,
which got his father's attention and support until he calmed down. If
the outbursts led to physical illness, his mother also gave him some
nurturing. Henry, two years older than Priscilla, became the family
whiner. Something was always wrong in his life. If he whined long
enough and consistently enough, either parent, but more frequently
his father, said, "Son, what in the world can I do to shut you up?" Then
he did it.

As you can imagine, Priscilla grew up into someone who
expected—and thus needed—to be a star at all times. Neither whining nor outbursts could threaten Priscilla's place at center stage in the
family as their beautiful and glowing star. Priscilla was described consistently as the light in her mother's life. When Tess said that, her husband smiled from ear to ear. After all, he was the one who finally gave
his beloved wife the daughter for which she yearned.

Willie was, in essence, a benevolent dictator who meant no harm
to those in his family. He had no understanding of boundaries and
when he insisted that all family vacations be taken together and even
refused Bruce and Henry's request that they go away to camp, he was
merely doing what his immigrant parents had done before him.

Camp would have been a marvelous experience for the two boys.
Henry could have learned to discuss things rather than complain.

Bruce could have learned there were better ways than temper tantrums to garner attention. Summer camp could have also helped Priscilla to know that the feelings of others mattered. At camp they could have had a myriad of experiences with other children and learned new ways of coping and existing. As it was, there was no break or release from the emotional abuse cycles that imprisoned the whole family.

As Priscilla, Bruce and Henry grew, so did the family business. After college, all three were expected to join the family business without further opportunity for graduate work and they each acquiesced. In the area of personal relationships, though Priscilla was beautiful, men lost interest in her quickly. In Bruce's words, "How many men would put up with what Henry and I have had to endure throughout our lives?" Bruce, the oldest, was so hurt by his mother that he lost interest in dating as a very young man—fearing the rejection he knew at two years old when Priscilla was born.

Henry, on the other hand, married in his senior year of college. He married a savvy, even-tempered woman who had a calming influence on him. In time, Henry grew to become the strength in the family business. It was Annabelle, Henry's wife, who first urged counseling about the family business interactions when their personal friction began demoralizing key staff members. Though the business was thriving, Bruce's ongoing tirades about everything and everyone were bad for employee morale and the effect of Priscilla's continued domination was hazardous.

It was at Henry's and Annabelle's insistence that all involved in this family and family business agreed to meet in my office one October afternoon four years ago—that is, all except Tess, the mother of the clan, who claimed that she was not part of the business and wasn't interested in therapy. Willie, however, uncharacteristically put his foot down, insisting that Tess also be present. She arrived reluctantly, knitting in hand.

Often as people mature, they become wiser and more sensitive. Such was the case with Willie. Willie opened our meeting saying that he worried about Priscilla and Bruce. "I love them and want them to have somebody in their lives after we go." Tess, knitting away, said, "Priscilla will be just fine." Bruce startled everyone in the room by screaming, "All my life, its been Priscilla, Priscilla and more Priscilla. What about me? Don't I exist?" Borrowing his mother's favorite martyred expression, he continued, "Or am I just chopped liver?"

Tess put her knitting down, demanding, "Willie, give him the tongue lashing he deserves." But Willie didn't say a word.

Bruce went over to his mother, sat in front of her and asked, "Why the hell don't you love me, too?"

Tess started to cry, seeming for the first time to hear the pain behind her son's anger. She touched his cheek and said quietly, "I'm sorry. I do love you. I'm sorry."

Bruce, whom the family had frequently seen angry but never tearful, began to cry. Henry became so flushed that Annabelle walked over to him and gently touched his shoulders. It was in this moment of catharsis that everything within this family and the way they talked to each other began to change. Still, it took more sessions for the family to work through the past. It was in the sixth session that Priscilla, now thirty-eight years old, asked, "How have you all put up with me? I've been such a goddamned spoiled brat."

In the months that followed, Priscilla married a man whom she had never noticed before, but who worked in the advertising division of the family business. She's far more thoughtful of other people, has given birth to two children and has maintained the best part of herself. On our last individual session, she told me, dimples flashing, "To my husband, I'm still the star and I love it. But I'm just no longer the kind of star who thinks that the stage is for her and her alone."

Henry and Annabelle continue in a stable and mutually satisfying relationship. As for Bruce, two years ago on a cruise, he fell in love.

The captain of the ship married the couple and after he called his parents, he called me and said, "There's nothing to be angry about anymore."

Willie has left his family business in the capable hands of his two sons and daughter. He and Tess are retired and live in Florida. Healthy and vibrant, they have become active in the Big Brother and Big Sister organizations in their community. At all times there is, in their words, at least one, sometimes more, "chosen" girls and boys in their world, along with six cherished grandsons.

The Emotional Abuse Cycle
of Rejection/Abandonment in the Workplace

My own early work history showed signs of the emotional abuse cycles I had suffered growing up. But as I learned later, this cycle had begun long before in my father's own past.

As a child, I learned to keep my thoughts to myself. I became a girl who loved to be in school—who loved her studies and took advantage of every activity offered. By my senior year of high school, I had been elected president of my school and president of my sorority. I also was elected homecoming queen, which meant that I went to every football game, although I never was interested in or enjoyed the game. I can still remember being crowned at half time one crisp autumn afternoon. There was cheering, noise and music, but I wanted only to run away. A voice in me kept whispering, What in the world are you doing here? *And another inner voice responded,* Anything is better than going home.

I kept hoping, however, that things would get better. I wanted my father's love so badly and I so yearned for him to be good to my mother, that I tried to accomplish the impossible by excelling in each course of study, moving from one endeavor to another, hoping to win his approval of me and loyalty to her. When neither happened, I would only try harder.

My honors and awards sometimes brought a smile to my mother, but con-
tinued to mean nothing to my father. I kept trying harder and harder—to
heal my mother and reach my father—until at last I began to draw strength
from the positive energy of other people who cared about me and could begin
to focus on the goals that meant the most to me.

Later I was able to understand that the approval my father was unable to
give me was something that he had never been able to win from his own father.
My father's father had a thriving fuel-oil business in Baltimore, but my father
was never interested in the business. A superb math student, he yearned to go
to college, but his father refused to help him. With his earnings from part-time
work, my father was able to enroll at the University of Maryland in College
Park and he began commuting from Baltimore. He could not afford room and
board or a car, so each day he hitchhiked to campus. One blustery week that
first winter, he developed frostbite and became very ill. His father "won": My
father never returned to college to complete his first semester.

From the moment he entered the family business, my father hated it. The
situation was exacerbated by the fact that his father was a tyrant who preferred
my father's younger brother, who also worked in the business. My father was far
more of a student than his brother and during the many years they worked
together, my father took every opportunity he could to vent his enormous frus-
tration and conflict by humiliating his brother. Sadly, he acted out his anger,
rather than working it out. In time, I was able to understand that my father's
self-loathing for giving up his dream undermined all I attempted. The more I
did to earn his love, the greater his contempt. Victimized by his own inner tur-
moil and lack of awareness, my father needed a scapegoat.

Many people go to work every day feeling angry or disappointed
with themselves. Some parents, usually without realizing it, establish
homes where their children are placed in constant competition for
their love with all who surround them: the other parent, siblings,
cousins and even friends. Parents may insist that their children be first

in everything without offering support, encouragement or praise. Instead they echo a constant refrain, "Why aren't your grades better?" and "Did you win?" These parents often deprive their children as adults of the capacity to experience any true confidence, satisfaction or happiness in the workplace—or in their lives.

Faced with relentless rivalries or a continuous barrage of criticism, some children just give up and refuse to try. Others are driven to stay on the run, ever achieving, but never feeling the permission and confidence to define what goals and pursuits will bring them satisfaction. Receiving no pleasure or satisfaction in anything they accomplish, they are constantly afraid that they will be unable to succeed in life's future challenges. They see everything in life as a contest, one they must win. For to "lose" means facing an inner emptiness—a feeling of nothingness and its accompanying fear, shame and sadness.

Those who make choices out of fear, anger, rejection or the lack of confidence that comes from overprotection will resent stronger colleagues who know they have the right to proceed without fear and know how to communicate like adults. In their professional lives, these worried people surround themselves with an inner circle of confidants who serve as an in-house cheering section to confirm their effectiveness. But ever on the run, ever dominated by anxieties about their next victory, those suffering in this way never feel satisfied enough to experience true fulfillment or joy. At work and at home, enough is never enough.

Managers or coworkers who were raised without being given permission to experience personal, individual joy and find a personal direction—who felt forced to constantly live to please and fulfill a parent—may seem charming and superficially supportive, when, in fact, they wish you to fail. It will shock and stun you when you realize that someone you viewed as a professional colleague was doing everything in his/her power to destroy your confidence or enjoyed taking potshots at you after you had experienced a success. These unhappy people hear their parents' familiar voices inside them forever echoing, "How can you leave me and be happy?" "How can you have joy when I have none?" "Why are you a loser?" "Why aren't you more of a winner?" Unable to know joy and happiness themselves, they resent, sometimes despise, those who do.

Chances are, if you work for someone, you were hired because you know how to do the job and you have kept the job because you do it well. No matter how difficult it may be, the hardest part of most work isn't the work itself—it's uneasiness or conflict with other personalities in the workplace. Many people come to the workplace with ingrained patterns of communication and reaction resulting from invisible cycles of emotional abuse and these play havoc with their effectiveness in dealing with colleagues and damage the potential success of their professional careers or businesses.

At any given time, almost everyone is worried about personal problems. Anyone who's having a health problem or a conflict with a partner or a child can come to work feeling distracted, impatient and angry. When these problems are temporary and not too serious, mature professionals usually manage to tend to the business at hand well enough without being rude or incommunicative. Others, however, such as victims of cycles of emotional abuse in their formative years, routinely communicate in ways that disrupt the workplace and threaten success.

In a healthy organization, whether it's a family or a global corporation, anxiety filters up, so that anyone who is unhappy about something can talk with the appropriate person to address the problem. In an unhealthy environment, anxiety filters from the top down, as executives and managers exercise control in unreasonable and inappropriate ways that create anger as well as intensify existing anxieties and pressures.

So many people in the workplace are talented, intelligent, motivated and energetic. However, what we don't have enough of in many workplaces is kindness, sincerity and compassion. Whenever and wherever possible, use your work and skills to offer understanding, hope and comfort to others.

Interests and work outside the home provide balance and enrich self-esteem. But work should not become our whole life. Find reliable mentoring, but remember that mentoring is not parenting. Looking for parenting from your employers or for brothers and sisters from your work colleagues, is a prescription for disaster. Keep your heart for your friends and your loved ones.

Work hard and work well. Then go home.

6

Community

It takes a village...

It's a paradox of human nature that in order to be fully independent and self-sufficient, each of us needs the support of others—a community of persons who believe in us, respect us and wish us well.

We experience two pivotal communities in life: the one into which we are born and the one we choose by creating it for ourselves. All children need a caring environment. Children who suffer from emotional abuse are especially blessed if they are born into a community where neighbors and friends are available to offer support and caring in appropriate ways, one in which faith communities and houses of worship are there to support and encourage and where schools provide teachers who not only are skilled in their subject matter, but also are kind and compassionate. This is especially important to a child who suffers emotional abuse.

The best schools encourage children to make the most of their individual potentials and teach that education is a lifelong process, one occurring in all facets of life. Especially when childhoods are painful, the concern of teachers and the nurturing philosophies of schools can help children believe in themselves, in spite of all they may be going through. In such environments, abused children are helped to accept reality and use what they have lived with and experienced to understand life and live creatively.

In adult life it is important to assess the community in which we live in order to see if it is the most productive environment for us— as well as those we love and care about or hope to love and care about in the future. Sometimes communities can be complemented and enriched. Sometimes it is necessary to make total changes.

An enriching community makes a great difference in one's life. A supportive community that offers opportunities for growth and welcomes you and your family can help you to compensate for any of life's necessary accommodations as well as the disappointments that are inevitable. Similarly, an enriching community makes your joys and successes even sweeter and more meaningful just as it makes tragedies such as illness and death more bearable.

One of the most important challenges before every one of us is how to find our own quality community, a place that feels right to us, a place in which we believe we can be accepted and grow. "People need people" as the song goes, but people are now often more isolated than ever.

The technological advances of our new century are dazzling. Yet technology has created our newest, sleekest and savviest isolation booths. At the same time that people are making more and more dot.com connections at Internet speed, many of us are becoming increasingly isolated: People don't even have to go to the library and see human faces as they pursue their educational goals. We don't have to reach out to a familiar voice on the phone (much less visit). We can just e-mail.

Fewer and fewer people are taking the time—insisting upon the time—for authentic personal connections. Those who lack these personal connections feel an emptiness that can never be filled by possessions and acquisitions. One result is that to ease their loneliness and its resulting anxieties, more and more adults and far, far too many children are turning to medication they most likely do not need and may not be able to give up.

I am not opposed to necessary medication to address chemical imbalance and stabilize a person. However, unless its use is accompanied by self-awareness that leads to inner strength, medication offers no real healing. One side effect of this kind of chemical manipulation sometimes is a hardening of attitudes toward others. Specifically, if a person fears his or her own vulnerability, medication may mask it rather than allow for understanding the problem. While on medication, which distances one from his or her feelings, a person may become cynical and dismissive when faced with vulnerability in another.

We humans are all vulnerable and understanding this can and should lead us to be kind and compassionate toward others. Increasingly, however, vulnerability is negatively viewed as being idealistic, naïve and weak. This is a destructive viewpoint that sabotages our ability to connect meaningfully with others and impairs healthy families and caring, supportive communities.

Emotional and physical isolation starve the spirit and create an emptiness that many people try to fill through materialism, addiction to food, sex, drugs or more medication. Yet even those who feel completely alone can discover that they can belong to caring communities that offer comfort, strength and hope.

Unless you take time to reflect on your life, you may not realize how many people have cared about you. If you think about it, you probably will remember in your community a relative, a neighbor, a religious leader, a counselor, a friend's mom or dad, a teacher or even a stranger who offered you kindness and who let you know that he or she believed in you. Once you have this support, it is yours forever. You can always call upon this reinforcement of your self-esteem and build upon it.

The Emotional Abuse Cycles of Rage and Rejection in Community: Rita's Story

Todd, my client Rita's husband, refused therapy to deal with his patterns of rage and rejection. Rita felt completely trapped in an abusive marriage and she felt so alone that she had begun to think that her life had no meaning and no value. However, in our work together she reflected on her earlier life. She remembered that though each of her parents treated her with rage and rejection, as did her husband, others in her community treated her differently.

"My piano teacher was so good to me," she told me. "I wasn't her best student, but she always believed in me."

As a child Rita had been emotionally battered by both parents and she subsequently chose an abusive husband. However, as she looked back on her girlhood and her young adult life, she recalled those who had had faith in her. As she remembered, she struggled to reconcile the conflicting images of herself that she saw reflected in the eyes of those who knew her best—images of a helpless child, a promising schoolgirl and a woman who had become afraid of her husband.

In remembering the kindness of her teacher, who had seen that she was bright and creative, Rita realized that it was the belief that others had in her that had given her the courage to question her relationship with Todd. When she began to see herself as her friends and others saw her, she discovered a reservoir of self-respect.

Rita worked hard to draw strength from those relationships and build her sense of worth. In time she succeeded. She also worked hard with Todd to end the abuse that was destroying their happiness. In this she could not succeed and finally she ended the marriage. Today she has a happy relationship with another man, a new community of friends and coworkers and a wonderful future.

Once we learn to believe in ourselves, it becomes possible to know when enough is enough: when it's time to end the emotional abuse, time to stop being hurt and time to move on to a new community of our own choosing and our own creation.

I think you're ready now to examine the possibilities, the potentials—the necessities!—of creating your own chosen community. To do this in the best possible way, let's look back at the yesterdays of your community life. Take time to think back about the community in which you were raised: Who made a difference in your life? Write about them in your journal in a quiet place. Read your entries aloud. Feel what you write. What experiences do you want to try to pass on to your own family? What people are you delighted to have left behind? What experiences do you never wish to repeat?

Now think about your community today. In times of happiness, to whom can you speak? In times of sadness, to whom can you turn? Are you welcomed in civic activities? Are you compatible with the values of those who lead your community? If you have an idea that you want to pursue or develop for the good of the community, are there places you feel you can go to relate your ideas?

A mature community is a group of neighbors, friends and colleagues who can express differences respectfully and who are open to the involvement of thoughtful, productive people who also care. Think about those people you know or work with in your community. Write about this in your journal. Read it aloud in private. Think honestly. Feel the truth of your words. Are you satisfied? Do you want some people off your list? If so, who? And why?

Getting Active in Our Communities

Communities are not just places from which we take. They are also places to which we give. Several years ago I had a challenging community experience with which all four of my children got involved. It was an experience that brought me to the board of a thriving neighborhood organization that has protected downtown

Philadelphia and helped to keep it vital—the Center City Residents Association. And it was an experience that led to many new friends and colleagues. Here's what happened:

For complicated bureaucratic reasons, our neighborhood trash collection day was changed from Tuesday to Friday evening. This meant that during synagogue services you'd hear the clanging of pick-up trucks. It also meant that those attracted to the interesting and unique restaurants in downtown Philadelphia would be obstructed by the trash pick-up trucks on Friday evenings and would step over scattered, leftover trash throughout the weekend.

You can understand that changing a bureaucratic decision can seem like you're dealing with immovable concrete. To make a long story short, through a combination of neighborhood meetings, letter writing and the force of the Center City Residents' Association, our objective was achieved. The Street Commissioner understood and was helpful—as soon as we could get him to answer my neighbors' and my ongoing letters. The letters were responded to, because a local newspaper editor, Dan Rottenberg, who was raised in New York City and is committed to city living, took all of my letters to various community leaders and published them along with their responses as a news story. Another very fortunate bit of luck was that some of the union members who had to agree to a pick-up change were the same ones I worked with when I led the union at an earlier job as Director of Family Life Education at Philadelphia's Jewish Family Services. They remembered that our work together had led to the medical benefits of the agency's clerical staff. And so a group of us in downtown Philadelphia took a lose/lose decision and through patience (it took two years!), collegiality, hard work and growing friendship, got the job done.

Just as those who have been impaired by emotional abuse can make home, professional, academic and business settings difficult, if not unbearable, community "leaders" can view their settings, organizations and boards as personal fiefdoms, feeling threatened if interested neighbors wish to and are invited to join their ranks. Such attributes of "leaders"—though they may be efficient and productive—squeeze the life and vitality from their settings.

Important hospitals, universities, schools, agencies and philanthropic resources with leaders or boards with this diminished caliber of "leadership" can inhibit the growth of their workplaces and, by extension, their communities if they fear democratic, interactive relationships.

The Global Village

Just as individuals compose a family, communities compose a society.

Recently, after the devastating attacks on the World Trade Center towers in New York City and the Pentagon in Washington, D.C., I was asked to write an article about the psychology of Osama Bin Laden. I understood the need for such a piece to appear. We have all been left bereft and heartbroken since September 11, 2001, searching for answers as to how such a violent tragedy could happen in a world that seemed so safe, in a life we had come to trust.

However, because of my life and work, I do understand the dynamics of the type of individual who is capable of such mass destruction. What makes a terrorist capable of such deeds? How do such monsters develop? It has nothing to do with wealth or native intelligence and everything to do with opportunities for healthy growth and expression offered by family and society, the very things you and I have been thinking over together through the chapters of this book. Those individuals without the opportunity to learn to think rationally and to accept and express themselves intellectually, emotionally and spiritually do not develop the confidence necessary to navigate the contradictions and confusions of life.

Frequently, these people turn to forms of fanaticism as sources of energy, purpose and direction. Though such individuals may mask it brilliantly, they are overwhelmed by the feelings of shame we have discussed. They live in terror that others will see how inadequate and diminished they feel. Their rage and feelings of envy and jealousy toward others overwhelm them. Unable to build their own homes, physically, emotionally and spiritually, they destroy the homes of others.

Many of these tyrants are terrified of female sexuality and female intimacy. Thus, some males of this type keep their women covered and deny them any normal outlets and the freedom to grow, learn and contribute to communities. For some, keeping plural wives is their way—not unlike the emotional abusers we have been reading about in love and work—of keeping women submerged and powerless, busy vying with the other women in the household for a husband's attention in order to survive.

Like the malevolent dictators we have discussed in past chapters, the only way such tyrants know how to live is through skillful, often charismatic, domination of others. Projecting their impotent rage on to scapegoats, they teach their followers, usually the poor and hopeless, to do the same.

Unable to fathom this perversion, Americans, like those in other civilized countries, ask what we have done to elicit such wrath. There are no rational answers. Tyrants project their hatred through false issues that they use to justify their actions. These "issues" are cover-ups for the shame they are feeling for being "less than" and emotionally impotent. They are used for one purpose only—as a weapon to project their hatred onto others.

A tyrant's hatred is not about limitations or mistakes made by a country like the United States, which admittedly are many and plentiful. Rather, such hatred is about a community of people and their capacity for compassion, love, productive work and success. It is about the abilities of a free country's citizens to think for themselves, speak their minds, disagree, discuss and reach consensus, however stormily. Terrorists hate those who live in freedom, because, with their emotional instabilities, they don't feel free to build their own homes and lives. They are the grand-scale, political amplification of all of the malevolent destroyers—the bullies and babies—we have spoken of in families, friendships and work settings.

It is very difficult to face reality when reality necessitates painful actions such as confronting a parent, partner or boss. The same courage is necessary in politics.

However, in facing the truth, victims of abuse, whether individuals or a country's population, must address their sadness, rage and feelings of violation. In this way they recover. For pain can always produce positive change and those who face the truth, no matter how painful or horrifying it is, emerge stronger, more resilient, more determined. However, without the kind of awakening that you have been experiencing on a personal level and our country is experiencing on a national one, the price to pay is eventual destruction.

Once the truth is faced on any level—be it personal or political—illusions disappear. At first, everything seems shaky, for nothing feels the same. Without the truth, "the same" would have continued to weaken and cripple. Through facing reality, change, always a constant, becomes positive. The pain accompanying truth, whether the truth resides in the personal or political, always leads to growth and is the only path to health and survival.

Whether an individual or a country is abused, it's never too late to take a positive approach to living, to claim one's rightful place in the community, to extend one's community or to start over and create a community of one's choice. It is never too late to face the manifestations of "wearing blinders" in every aspect of life—and to remove them. In a stable family, community and country, there are always

ways to reclaim one's individual self. There are always ways to find ful-fillment and happiness. And if a family, community and country are not stable, there are always ways for them to become so. For in the hearts and souls of all those emotionally imprisoned, even if their minds have never been exposed to dignity and truth, there is always the longing for the sunlight of love and freedom. As Montaigne wrote, "My reason is not obliged to bow and scrape, that is for my knees."

If one has ever taken the time to look at our vast heavens on a beautiful evening, one cannot help but ask: "How can the only life be ours?" From this perspective, our Earth is both small and vulnerable; one cannot help but conclude that we are all in this life together. Caring about the opportunities of all who live here becomes not only a right attitude, it becomes a necessary one. For unless all people know the joys of freedom and expression without abuse and tyranny, we will not be safe. Nor will the world's children, grandchildren or any who follow.

In this critical time of rethinking the past both as individuals and citizens, think about positive contributions you wish to make to a community of your choice or to our global village. Remember that a community can be of your choosing and that your options for the gifts of giving and sharing are enormous. There are so many ways you can contribute. The important thing is to get involved and care.

You may never be told of the life saving affirmation your gen-erosity of time and spirit brings. However, your gifts will live on in many unimagined but beautiful ways. They will offer hope. They may very well save lives.

In my own life, reflections on community have brought me much insight...

My earliest neighborhood was a lively section of Baltimore called Lower Park Heights, a place that was home to many religions. As I've said, from ages three to six, while my mother tried to regain her health, though she, too, lived in this neighborhood, I did not live with her. During these years I alternated between the homes of my maternal grandfather and paternal grandmother. Each was widowed and lived on the same block. I now know that my maternal grandfather had never liked my father and paternal grandfather, who was a tyrant. He was, however, a tyrant, who had achieved financial success for his family.

My maternal grandfather, on the other hand, had a wealthy and privileged life in Poland, but as a young man he fled to this country with his manservant to escape an arranged marriage with a woman he did not love. A brilliant and educated man, but used to the life of a gentleman, my mother's father never earned a good living. Above all, my mother grew up yearning for financial security, never realizing the price she would eventually pay.

During those early years, to escape my loneliness and fears about my mother's health as well as my grandfather's active and verbal dislike for my father, I busied myself by making friends in the houses nearby. All along the block of marble-stepped row houses, children played together and traded comic books and movie magazines. Neighborhood children went en masse to bingo games at St. Ambrose. My friend Ileen and I adored stopping at the local deli, Cooper's, to buy little fish cakes called "coddies" smothered with mustard or browsing in a little variety store that was owned by a couple we knew only as Mr. and Mrs. Charlie. Each year my friend Rosemary invited me to her church bazaar, where we delighted in the traveling Ferris wheel.

Rosemary had an amazing collection of photographs of movie stars that she carefully cut out from her trove of movie magazines. She could sense whenever I was sad and at these times she always brought me into her home to show me pictures of her favorite stars: Shirley Temple, Lana Turner, Susan Hayward, Betty Grable and Margaret O'Brien. My relationship with Rosemary was very important. On so many evenings, after I'd spent the whole afternoon at her house, her mother would set a place for me at the supper table.

One summer day, Rosemary told me that something awful had happened to her next-door neighbors, Mr. and Mrs. Bernstein: "Mrs. Bernstein's baby was born dead." Rosemary and I were horrified. We didn't know what to do. Day after day we saw Mrs. Bernstein sitting alone on her front porch in a rocking chair, speaking to no one. As the warm weeks passed, she seemed to grow paler each day.

Then one afternoon I walked to the corner grocery store and asked Mrs. Charlie if there were any cards about a baby who died. Mrs. Charlie asked no questions and gave me the only sympathy card she had in the store. I took it to Rosemary and we signed our names below a beautiful picture of what I know today was the Virgin Mary. That evening we slipped the card under Mrs. Bernstein's front door.

If Mrs. Bernstein, an Orthodox Jew, was in any way offended by our choice of cards, she surely didn't show it. The next morning, when Rosemary and I walked past her house, she was waiting on her porch with a pitcher of lemon-ade. She called to us and gave us each a glass of lemonade and a big hug. Later, after Rosemary left to go home for lunch, Mrs. Bernstein gently placed me on her lap, put her arms around me and silently rocked us in her chair. Just as she must have guessed how desperately I missed my mother, I knew how she longed for her lost child. On that afternoon I understood that somehow we were helping each other.

While the neighbors on my street, Oswego Avenue, were wonderfully sensi-tive to me, my experience in kindergarten was not as good. I was by no means a pretty child and was pudgy and awkward. While the other children who lived on the block had mothers to care for them, to plait their hair or curl it, to choose matching hair ribbons, to carefully iron their blouses and dresses, I must have been a sight to behold in wrinkled cotton shirts and mismatched skirts and socks. My curly hair was unruly and, to make matters worse, I was myopic (which was discovered in the third grade when I was given glasses).

My father, through political connections, arranged for me to start kinder-garten earlier than before the normal time. From the first moment my two kindergarten teachers saw me and contrasted me with the beautifully cared for other girls (and boys) in our class, they disliked me. To take matters from bad to worse, their favorite students were those who could sing and draw and I could do neither. So every day at recess, while the others would go out and play, those who could not sing or draw had to practice. "You'll stay in until you get it right," we three failures were told, punished along with those who were put in the corner for not getting to the bathroom on time. I was afraid to speak of my failure to my grandfather, with whom I was living at the time. He had walked me to school on my first day of kindergarten, telling me the importance of an education. I loved him dearly and felt awful that I was letting him down.

I was delighted and relieved that even though I never learned to draw or sing—unlike two of my fellow failures—I graduated from kindergarten. (After my second marriage, I learned that it was a hearing impairment that kept me from any musical talent whatsoever. I learned to lip read, study body language and listen very carefully without ever realizing why. As for my poor drawing skills, I have no excuse.)

During the summer my parents and I moved to Mount Washington, a suburb of Baltimore, I lived in terror about starting the first grade. I certainly didn't want a teacher like my two former ones. Of all horrors, I learned on my first day of school that my new teacher, Miss Miller, could sing and draw beautifully. On our first propitious day of class, we were asked to draw something. Perhaps because I hoped to journey someplace better, I drew a train.

The next day when I arrived at school, much to my surprise my train was one of those selected for the bulletin board. Miss Miller's kindness to me changed my life and my views about school. She even suggested that I join the glee club, diplomatically asking that I just move my lips for the high notes (which I now know I never could hear). She must have felt badly about her request, because she suggested that I announce all the programs.

Another joy in my young life was my relationship with my grandmother. She was strong and spunky and she loved to tell me about her antics with her older sisters and brothers on the farm in Lithuania where she was born. I was still very young and we were in her kitchen drinking hot spiced tea when she told me of how she made the trip to her new home in America when she was seventeen, a journey she made alone.

She loved to listen to my own stories about school, friends and anything else I chose to share. Whenever I told her anything that troubled me, I always felt better. During these conversations, she would nod her head in rapt attention as she sipped her tea or coffee, depending upon her mood. Once I asked her to tell me the purpose of life.

"The purpose, darling, is your journey" is the only response she made. But she promised, "Do not be afraid of life without me. My love will be yours forever."

It was my grandmother who first taught me that it is a feeling of self-worth, of inner dignity, that keeps us going when life is toughest. She told me of her own longing for an education while growing up, an impossible dream for a girl who lived far from the city. She spoke lovingly of her parents and relatives and how they sent her to the safety of her cherished "new country" shortly before they were murdered in the pogroms that engulfed Central Europe in the early 1900s.

History has shown that even conquered and enslaved people can maintain a sense of self-worth, providing that someone has expressed it to them sometime during their lives. Of all gifts, I believe this is the most priceless component of love and my grandmother's greatest gift to me. My grandmother also taught me that everyone has private battles and because of this everyone should try to be as kind as possible to others. She tried to teach me to seek out relationships with those who want to love and work hard, but for whom control and ambition are not the paramount drives.

Whenever times were hard, my grandmother insisted upon facing reality and remembering the happy times and the people she loved. During difficult periods in my own life, I often think about how my grandmother would counsel me and I imagine what she would say: "In each life, there's a lot of lemons and we have to learn to make lemonade." She'd add that when you've tried and tried to make lemonade, but just can't, then it's time to throw out the damn lemons, *go to a movie or have your hair done. She also knew that whenever there is water in a glass, the glass is partly full. I can still see her sipping her steaming tea or coffee and hear her wise, warm, reassuring words. I've never stopped missing her, but because of the love we shared, she's always with me and my children. Our love has made her immortal.*

I still have the porcelain kitchen canisters that my grandmother brought to America from Lithuania. The first thing I do in any home that is mine is place those containers in the kitchen. I remember my grandmother using them as she cooked and I firmly believe her love resides in the containers for flour, coffee, tea and sugar. In times of trouble I go into my kitchen, brew a cup of tea and give myself time to think. After this I always feel stronger and able to face what is necessary.

For each of us, community is essential. A caring community can give a child hope and can greatly compensate for the love children do not receive from their parents in their formative years. Even those who don't have this support can find it, once they learn to recognize which attitudes and behaviors serve them well and which ones don't. Those who understand this need can create chosen families and communities that will support them at every step of their journeys.

As children and throughout our adult lives, the communities we choose to join and the ones we create—with our families, our neighbors, our coworkers and our friends—make life fulfilling.

7

How to Start Healing

It takes enormous courage to face the truth.

Perhaps you chose this book because your life feels joyless or you feel numb and don't know why or you feel pain which you have tried desperately to push down through constant motion, addictive behavior or relentless ambition. It may be that your pain has led to depression, anxiety attacks, eating disorders and other negative physical and emotional manifestations. It may be that you have only superficial, unsatisfying relationships and are not really close and intimate with another adult. It could be that your loneliness is unbearable.

Having come this far in our work together, hopefully your understanding of the cycles of emotional abuse, which most likely happened in your childhood and have continued until now, has increased greatly. Through this knowledge you have developed more awareness about the reasons for your pain. You are beginning to see how these past cycles have affected your choices and have hurt and imprisoned you. Whereas before you may have said about certain relationships, "I just keep hoping things will change," you now know much more about whether they really can change or whether clinging to illusionary hope is your way of deluding yourself and not facing reality.

Once you study the patterns of self-perpetuating abuse pervading your life and realize the impact they have had on you, you won't be able to push down the pain or delude yourself as easily. You will feel anxiety and its intensity may be frightening to you. Remember though, internal pain is a signal that something is hurting you. It also is a signal from your inner self, calling out—sometimes demanding—to be heard. Remember that allowing yourself to feel the pain is a sign of hope. Identifying and facing its causes is an act of courage.

Sometimes pain is unavoidable. The pain of illness and the loss of those we love are painful aspects of life that cannot be avoided. Part of life's challenge, however, is to avoid the pain that can be avoided and leave the pain that can be eliminated behind you.

For instance, the pain of being used or treated rudely by friends can be eliminated. The pain that comes from not recognizing warning signs of emotional abuse can be eliminated. The pain of living without intimacy can be eliminated. The pain of being with a partner who shames and humiliates you can be eliminated. The pain of not righting a situation that you know is not serving you well can be eliminated.

However, eliminating these agonies is not easy. Righting a situation that is not serving you well can be very distressing, but this distress will lead to healing. Like labor pains, this pain is a sign of a new beginning, perhaps a rebirth. The truth of this is expressed in the Chinese language by the symbolic letters for "crisis" which have two meanings: "danger" and "opportunity." We all know individuals who have left unhappy job situations for example and seem to have changed completely or people who chose to relocate to new communities, ones that brought out the best in them.

No one reaches maturity without experiencing internal upheavals that cause unhappiness and leave emotional wounds. We all develop ways to protect ourselves from being aware of these wounds and feeling their pain. We try to fool ourselves or we try to avoid certain behaviors, interactions or attitudes that remind us of old injuries.

Ironically, the defenses we create to protect ourselves can destroy our relationships and shatter our dreams. Unless we understand why and how emotional abuse cycles pervaded our childhood homes, we cannot adopt positive new attitudes and behaviors. Part of maturity is to understand how we feel about what happened to us in the past and no longer feel like victims because of these events. In other words, for each of us the real challenge in life is to face reality.

Leaving behind the role of victim is a difficult task for someone whose self-esteem has been threatened by shame and humiliation. Building on the theories of my mentor, Dr. Eli Marcovitz, there are some differences worth noting between shame and humiliation. When someone insults us publicly—*i.e.*, a teacher tells us we are stupid or a boss rudely criticizes our careful work—one feels humiliation. However, those who were raised in homes where there were one or more cycles of emotional abuse experience constant shame. Humiliation is a result of outside forces—circumstances and people around us who are unkind, unjust or rude. Humiliation can also come about as we experience the results of our own poor judgment.

Shame, however, comes from within. Children enduring emotional abuse do not develop the necessary pride to cope with life's humiliations, difficulties and obstacles. Without these coping mechanisms, these children grow to maturity feeling shame—believing they are "less than," inferior, unworthy of love. They not only feel inferior, they live in fear that others will discover their perceived deficiencies. As a result, they both avoid facing their faults and run from situations in which their weaknesses may be illuminated for others to see.

The opposite of shame is a sense of self-worth and self-value or, in a word, dignity. In my first book, *Whoever Said Life Is Fair?*, I discussed my belief—as explored by Eli Marcovitz—that nurturing one's dignity is necessary to have a truly meaningful and fulfilling existence. Without dignity, a person is emotionally vulnerable to others and is easily manipulated and abused. It is clear that such a person

would have difficulty finding joy in many aspects of life. Indeed, true
emotional health and well-being cannot be achieved or maintained
without dignity.

Dignity, as Eli Marcovitz describes it, is "the development of standards, ideals, ethics and responsibilities, as well as the ability to stand off
and evaluate oneself with justice and humor." He further defines dignity
as a combination of pride and humility, pride being an inner feeling of
self-worth and confidence and humility being the awareness of one's
own powers *and* limitations. In this case, "limitations" is not meant to
denote feelings of being "less than" or certainty that you will never
achieve your goals. (Such feelings and convictions are evidence of
shame, its resulting low self-esteem and defeating relentless perfection-
ism.) Instead, accepting limitations means knowing who you are and
where your vulnerabilities lie. You must learn to accept what you don't
yet or may never know. You must learn to recognize how slowly you
may have to go to get where you hope to be. Finally, you must do your
best to accept and endure what this journey of life requires of us all.

Humility is an essential part of dignity. Without it, you are left only
with pride, which, on it's own, may border on boastful arrogance or
worse—not a trait most people associate with "dignity." Humility tem-
pers pride. Together, they result in an individual who is both confident
and believes in himself, but is also aware of and realistic about his limitations. On the other hand, without this awareness, without humility,
the individual elevates himself to a God-like level of perfection and
invulnerability. Such a person thinks he is better than others and will
likely emotionally abuse the people in his life. These are the tyrants and
dictators in families, workplaces, communities and society at large.
They do exactly as they please, take what they want—often charm-
ingly—with no regard for anyone but themselves, making life intolerable for others as they move toward their goals. Such Malevolent
Dictators may not literally believe they are gods, but they certainly act
as if they are perfect beings cast in His image.

Thus the importance of humility cannot be underestimated. Humility comes to those who face reality and in so doing feel the worth of their humanity, but also know their limitations, including the reactive patterns to which they may be prone. It is this state of dignity, a combination of pride and humility—a fair assessment of who we are, what our strengths and our weaknesses are and where we hope to go—that we are working toward together through understanding the cycles of emotional abuse and the impact of these cycles on our own lives.

Dignity is acquired in early childhood, but it transforms with time and experience. For example, the natural dignity of a child enjoying exploration and learning new skills is different from that of a teenager expanding her world view. The confident dignity of a man or woman of middle years is different from the quiet dignity of those who have gained wisdom over the course of long, fulfilling lives. Remember, it is never too late in life's journey to acquire dignity.

There are five concepts with which you must work to further your task of healing from emotional abuse. They are:

Humiliation: *Unkind or unjust treatment by others in our past and present lives.*

Shame: *The belief that we have a weakness or inferiority—are less than, unworthy, unlovable—carried over from the past.*

Dignity: *A sense of self-worth that lends purpose and joy to living.*

Pride: *An inner feeling of confidence, an awareness of our powers, an ability to use them responsibly in work, friendship and love.*

Humility: *Recognition of one's limitations, in terms of knowing who we are, what we don't know, asking for help and seeing others as worthy of respect.*

You have been reading about the five cycles of emotional abuse that consistently, generation after generation, rob human beings of dignity. In the case studies we have reviewed, you have seen how inner feelings of shame and the resulting feelings of worthlessness that are indicative in cycles of emotional abuse, coupled with the humiliation and ridicule that parents, teachers, peers and the world can bring on, may cause people to fall through the cracks and/or perpetuate self-destructive patterns of behavior.

In order to maintain your dignity or develop it if emotional abuse has been part of your life, it is necessary to be able to stand up for yourself. If you have not learned how to believe in yourself and, when necessary, stand up and fight for yourself in childhood, it takes great fortitude to learn how to stand up for yourself later. You may sense what you view as a contradiction in the cycle of rage—or when a reaction to other cycles is rage. You may be saying: "Those who are always angry do speak up and speak out." And you are correct. Such people do make noise, but in nonproductive, unfulfilling ways—ones that estrange them from families and friends in their personal worlds.

Those caught in the cycle of rage do not know how to communicate effectively and maturely and are imprisoned by their baby/bully tirades in their professional lives as well. Either they cannot hold jobs or they dominate others who, eventually, come to hold them in disregard and view them with contempt. The shame of those in this cycle of rage or in other cycles who react to their emotional abuse with explosive anger is as deep and depleting as those imprisoned by the perpetuation of the cycles of enmeshment, rejection/abandonment, complete neglect and extreme overprotection.

By now, you have seen that change is possible. Although you have read how others did it, you may still have lingering doubts and questions about your ability to break a cycle or cycles of emotional abuse, apprehensions that come in the form of unspoken mental attitudes.

These attitudes manifest as fears of what will happen if you do manage to stand up for yourself, such as:

I don't have the right to speak up.

I will be punished.

I'll lose my friends.

I'll lose my loved ones.

I won't know what to do with anything better.

I can't change things anyway.

Without the ability to assert ourselves in order to achieve the dignity of which we were deprived when the cycles of emotional abuse were imposed on us, human beings feel helpless, dependent, anxious and depressed. When children are dominated—encroached upon in personal choices and expressions—they become inhibited in their ability to stand up for themselves. The resulting shame makes them more susceptible to humiliation and ridicule from the outside world, where they are often exploited and used by others for their own purposes. Such individuals are constantly frightened that if they speak up, they will be rejected or attacked by those they love, depend upon and need. With each episode of humiliation and ridicule, of domination and exploitation, they feel greater worthlessness, unlovability and inferiority. With each episode, their emotional inertia is amplified.

To rid yourself of this inertia caused by emotional abuse, to stop it in your own world and not perpetuate it in your children, it is necessary to determine to change. In our work together as you read this book, your understanding of your past emotional abuse has undoubtedly grown. My goal in this chapter and the one to follow is to help you translate that understanding into a belief in yourself and your ability to carve out new ways of feeling good about yourself and the knowledge that you can act assertively and productively to make change. In other words, to help you do something—anything—that will lead to a new path, a new way. This change will be a gift to yourself, a gift you will pass on to your loved ones, so that they, too, can free themselves. Thus the cycle of emotional abuse will end.

Also, before we proceed any further, I want to make one point clear, perhaps clearer than I have made it up until now. Most parents never wish or mean to hurt their children. Most do the best they can, never wanting to inflict pain. When parents do hurt their children, it is usually unknowingly. However, though most would never call what they do harmful and have no realization of what they do or why, some parents emotionally abuse in exactly the way they were abused or through a different reactive pattern.

As you read, bear in mind my definition for mental health: knowing yourself and doing your best not to inflict your emotional limitations on others and being able to apologize when and if you do. To get close to loved ones and our children puts us in the position of being able to hurt. But recognition can mean change. Those, however, who don't care how they treat others or enjoy hurting others are the people in life who should be avoided or, when this is not possible, buffered.

As children grow, no matter how secure their home, they will have fears about the constancy of love surrounding them, their places in their families, their rivalries, their enemies, their angers, their futures. With the exercises you've used in this book, I believe you're moving toward self-insight. Such insight can, if you allow it, lead to empathy; through this process you've begun to understand that the abuse you endured is exactly like or in reaction to what those who hurt you experienced in their own childhood. You also now understand that these cycles perpetuate themselves from one generation to the next and that it's up to you to set yourself free and live differently.

This understanding and empathy can lead you to know how to proceed: Should you communicate with those who have hurt you or is it best to work it out within yourself, realizing that direct communication would be nonproductive and abusive? Specifically, it is wise for those who have been hurt by their parents to take time to consider whether their parents hurt them because of their own neediness or because they are malicious.

If the cause is neediness, changes in the son's or daughter's behavior can remedy the situation, though the resolution may be painful. As children grow more independent and confident, they can educate their parents to behave differently toward them and let go emotionally. Needy parents probably will not like to see their children changing their behavior or calmly insisting upon more space. They may become angry and lash out unfairly—just as their own parents reacted to them or probably would have reacted had they requested room for their own individual growth—but they will not become vindictive or seek revenge. If they do not want to lose their relationships with their children, they will learn to treat their children with respect, even if they remain upset or hurt, because they cannot understand their children's need for independence. Remember that all of us resist change; it's part of human nature.

Most parents truly wish their children well. There are, unfortunately, exceptions. Some people—because of deeply rooted illnesses or character flaws, ones which they cannot or do not choose to see and remedy—do not wish their children happiness. These parents may refuse to express respect as their children reach toward maturity. Instead, they can become malicious or vindictive if they sense any attempts by their children to separate from them. Parents who seek revenge if their children behave in more mature ways—parents who say hurtful things if they begin to lose control of their children—may need to be kept at some distance if their sons and daughters are to have mature lives of their own.

Parents deserve respect and compassion throughout their lives, but honoring our parents does not mean allowing ourselves to be abused. It means setting limits. Sometimes it may even be necessary to break all contact with one or both parents. When estrangement with parents is a strong possibility, one must make a hard choice: either eliminate any expectation of a mature and mutual relationship and live with and buffer the frustration, anger and turmoil of being in contact with them or work out as well as possible the guilt and loss of ending contact.

Mature adults accept responsibility for their own lives and they blend the good experiences they were given as children together with those experiences they create for themselves in order to live the most fulfilling lives possible. We all endure some degree of pain and disappointment—rejection, hostility, material and emotional deprivation—all the sad and desperate situations that are part of living. However, one can learn to see the difference between "some degree" of pain and an ongoing and persistent cycle (or cycles) of emotional abuse. A combination of insight and love can dissolve the aggression and hate and relieve the guilt they bring.

Should you confront your father about having humiliated you as a child? Can you stop blaming your mother for belittling you? The following pages will help you find the right answers, ones that will help rid you of feelings of shame and their accompanying feelings of helplessness, worthlessness and inertia.

As Jean-Paul Sartre once said, "Freedom is what we do with what's been done to us."

8

Breaking the Five Cycles
of Emotional Abuse

Today is the first day of the rest of a better life.

As you have read this book, no doubt certain cycles seemed very real and apropos to you, while others may have seemed important, but somehow not as relevant. It is crucial to pay attention to your gut reaction, because we often hide salient facts from ourselves, even those of us who are trying to heal! It is paying attention to your gut reaction that allows an inner voice, which may have been stifled by one or more cycles of emotional abuse, to emerge. This "voice" is a combination of feelings, life experiences and acquired knowledge. It increases the power of intuition and the capacity for courage. It helps you not give up until you are able to work hard and love well enough to make good things happen. It is your truest life guide. Listen to your inner voice, which has been emerging as we have been working together.

Remember the five cycles of emotional abuse. In the exercise which follows, I want you to put two stars next to the cycle or cycles that seem the most relevant to you and one star next to the cycle or cycles that seem to relate to your situation, even if they are not as powerful as the others. Remember life does not occur in or within neat lines. Life is messy. So there may well be overlap of differing cycles.

Five Cycles of Emotional Abuse Exercise

_____ Rage

_____ Enmeshment

_____ Extreme Overprotection

_____ Rejection/Abandonment

_____ Complete Neglect

On the following pages, I will offer specific words for the victims or abusers caught up in these cycles. Bear in mind that you may be both a victim of emotional abuse and an abuser. That is, you may have endured emotional abuse and now treat others as you were treated. It is very common for an individual who has suffered the impact of a cycle of emotional abuse to then, without realizing it, become one of its proponents. Unfortunately, these destructive patterns of emotional abuse are so well ingrained that they can become instinctive.

Those who get great pleasure and satisfaction abusing others won't want to change their sadistic behavior. However, many people caught in the cycle of hurting others as they have been hurt know something is wrong, something that they want to change. Nevertheless, they can't name it, can't define it and, therefore, can't change it. As Joelle, a recent client of mine, put it, "I'm here, because I think that unknowingly I've done things to harm my children, my husband, my friends. I want to understand myself and I want to stop these negative actions."

While reading this book, you may have suspected that you have been the abuser in one or more of these cycles and that you have kept the cycle going without consciously seeing or knowing your actions. You may feel that while you know what you have been reading about cycles of emotional abuse is true for you and about you, you don't have the knowledge or the resolve to begin doing things differently. I want to assure you that you do have the power. And if right now you believe you can't find the strength in or for yourself to use your power, I promise you that you are wrong—very wrong indeed.

The thing to keep in mind with any destructive cycle of behavior, as you think about trying to break it, is that the behaviors and attitudes are "familiar." The word familiar comes from the same root as the word "family"; we learned these familiar behaviors and attitudes within our families, at the same time, or before, we learned to walk! Such "programming" cannot be wiped away in an hour. However, this is not something to feel badly about. Remember my comments on the organic nature of the cycle of emotional abuse, in the introduction to this book: This is the natural way that things will go until you are able to find the strength to do things differently. This is the way things unfold; this is, as the physicists say, "the curve of binding energy." Rather than despair, I want you to look closely at my recapitulation of the five cycles and my advice for how to break the chains that bind you. And know one more thing: In doing this brave work, I salute you.

Breaking the Emotional Abuse Cycle of Rage

If you have been the victim of the emotional abuse cycle of rage, you may not know how to ask for what you really want. You may not be in touch with what you desire or need in this life and you probably have great difficulty validating those needs. In addition, you may be frightened, have a quick "startle response" and be terrified of your own uncontrollable temper. It is very likely that you live with a feeling of doom that the world or a situation will turn against you abruptly, through no fault of your own.

If you have been the recipient of excessive anger you may feel like "slinking away" from situations or feel unable to meet anyone's eyes. And yet, it is what you carry with you from your past more than likely that is creating the problems you may be experiencing in the present.

For the next three weeks I want you to complete the following "homework assignments." Afterward, you will write in your journal about what you felt and did during this time. As before, after you have finished writing, please read your journal aloud in a private place, where you can let yourself feel your words and the reactions within you.

Changing Self-concept Exercise for Victims of Rage

1) Find a room with a door that locks and sit down in it alone, having made sure the door is locked. Tell yourself that you are safe. No one can come in this room without your permission. Stay there past the time that the novelty has worn off, breathing deeply and really feeling that you are alone, you are safe and no one can hurt you. Carry this room with you when you do choose to leave, as a place inside you that you can return to whenever you want.

2) Try going back to that locked room (in actuality now) at a time when you feel most distraught about present circumstances. See how quickly the feeling of safety allows you to return to a more reasonable assessment of what is currently transpiring. Know that you have the right to be free from harm, to remove yourself whenever you want from anger or verbal abuse.

3) As victims of the emotional abuse cycle of rage most likely have the lowest self-esteem of any of the five cycles (while victims of the other end of the spectrum, neglect, may have the least sense of purpose), make a list of ten characteristics about yourself that you really like. You can, if you'd like to, make a list of three characteristics that you don't like as much to lend some balance to your self-portrait; the point is to be positive about who you are and who you can become. Carry this list around with you, although you don't have to show it to anyone.

4) Assume that the next person you meet for the first time knows nothing about how you were perceived growing up,

that he or she has never heard any of the insults leveled at you, has no inclination that you are anything but a loving, capable and desirable person.

5) Try this assumption next on someone whom you know quite well. For instance, when a disagreement breaks out, instead of retreating to your normal defenses of cringing or possibly breaking into a rage yourself and attacking another as cruelly as you were once attacked, carry on as if everything has always been fine and will continue to be so. Regard the argument as a simple misunderstanding that can be worked out; it is not a matter of life or death or "win above all." Continue the argument to its conclusion with the same respect for another's humanity that you are working toward for yourself.

As a victim of the emotional abuse cycle of rage, you most likely feel awful when you are exposed to insults, obscenities and out-of-control anger. Though you try to hide it from others, unless you are a malevolent dictator, you feel doubly awful and deeply ashamed if or when your own rage bubbles up and eventually explodes. If you are propagating the cycle of rage, you probably feel ashamed and out of control about your inability to stop hurting the ones you love. The first thing to realize when trying to break any destructive cycle of behavior is the tremendous negative impact it has had on you and those about whom you care. In the case of victims of rage and anger, this may be fairly obvious: Problems can never be maturely addressed and solved in such scenarios. Most or all of the members of the household may dissolve into tears every night, hearts may be broken, resentments may grow and resolution remains impossible.

If you are prone to angry outbursts, you will need to put an internal check on your behavior when acting out. Anger management seminars can be very useful in dealing with this problem. So can a reconstructed attitude. Identify that you are angry. Tell yourself you can handle your feelings. Try to view the one with whom you are angry in a positive light. Tell yourself that he or she means you no harm (if you find this observation untrue, you must stop and consider your options). Understand what is making you angry: What has the person said? What has the person done? What is the general circumstance you both may be in? With these recognitions come choices. You can allow your anger free reign—with all of the volcanic rhetoric and wounding that your words may cause—or you can bury it. However, if you choose suppression, your anger will probably come out later in unhealthy ways, like belittling insults (either constant or out of the blue), teasing, stonewalling, withdrawal or other passive-aggressive behaviors. A better approach is to resolve to stand your ground and speak for yourself about your truth. Another approach is realizing that in some cases healthy dialogue would be nonproductive. In this case, you can work your anger out within yourself and consider your options regarding the relationship.

Remember my earlier comments about the bully and the baby? The bully, the loudmouth, the rageaholic, is actually a frightened, insecure child who is terrified that his or her words won't have meaning or be taken seriously if they don't come out violently or in an overpowering fashion. These individuals view rage as the cover for an inherent shame for being deficient, unlovable, unworthy, "less than."

The realistic solution for such dictators is self-knowledge: When you scream and carry on, you are less likely than ever to be heard. You can count to ten or twenty or fifty when you are able to identify the angry impulse. After that time, you will most likely be better able to express your dissatisfaction rationally, which gets results! And for those people or situations where calm, rational discussion is impossible, you must then assess your options.

One more suggestion: Apologize to those you have hurt through your rage. Tell them you are working to change your behavior and reactions. This acknowledgment will make an enormous difference in your life and the lives of loved ones. In this way you will have done your part to end the cycle of rage begun in your own childhood, the one you have perpetuated.

Breaking the Emotional Abuse Cycle of Enmeshment

The cycle of enmeshment is one of the hardest to detect. Because everything seems so normal and loving to an outsider, the family dynamic may simply seem to be one of unusual closeness and love. However, if there is no room for privacy or individuality for each family member, the family unit may actually become a destructive, smothering entity. When you look very closely, you will find irritation, games, traps and a desire to exclude those outside the family unit or blame them for any problems within the family.

If you have been the victim of enmeshment, you may feel that separating from your family of origin or, by extension, from an unhealthy love relationship or work experience will literally result in your death. After all, you have been taught that you must depend on one or more individuals, usually your parents and later a wage-earning spouse or partner or perhaps even a boss, for your very livelihood.

Place yourself in an imaginary picture surrounded by those you now realize are creating a prison that you fear leaving. What would happen if you separated from them and didn't die? How would you feel then? My guess is you would feel free. And what, if you did extricate yourself, would you feel looking back on the relationships? Perhaps you would recognize that you had entrusted too much power and authority to the individuals from whom you have to separate. Perhaps you will recognize that you looked to them to think and plan for you and that any rebellion you chose to act upon was one that hurt you through wrong relationships, addictive traps and continued self-doubt. You will no doubt begin to realize that you fear not leaving them, but your freedom. You fear this, because you do not believe that

you will know how to live in a self-sufficient way once you set yourself free.

My goal is to help you know that you can, must and will become
a whole individual person. You do not have to burn bridges or unnec-
essarily destroy relationships by becoming free. Nevertheless, relationships without proper boundaries and healthy respect are paralyz-
ing affairs that do not lead to individuals manifesting their truest
potential. The goal must be to set yourself free. For if you do not, you
face a living death. Enmeshment is a death-in-life situation that children, if you have them, will perpetuate.

For the next three weeks I want you to complete the following
"homework assignments," after which you will write in your journal
about what you felt and did during this time. You know my recom-
mendation: A private place for journal reading, experiencing your
body language, letting yourself feel.

Changing Self-concept Project for Victims of Enmeshment

1) Plan one step of freedom for yourself—take a trip, a course
   at the community center, a new experience that will enrich
   you. Ideally this will be something in which you have always
   had an interest, but which no one in your family has ever
   dreamed of doing. Participate in this activity without telling
   anyone in your immediate environment, not to hold an
   unhealthy secret, but to begin to carve out some area that is
   just yours.

2) Now, tell one family member, friend or co-worker with
   whom you have had enmeshment problems what you have
   done. See whether his or her reaction surprises you. Note if
   you start to doubt your own experience that arose during the
   activity, because it does not correspond with what your
   friend, family member or associate expected of you. This may

serve as a useful model for how you lose sight of your own values and feelings when more emotionally difficult situations occur.

3) For the next exercise you will need to copy the questions which follow into your journal. At the top of the page place the name of an important person in your life who imprisons you. It could be a mother, father, sister, brother, boss, husband, wife, co-worker or friend. Look at the questions as you copy them into your journal, reading them aloud. Then write your responses, paying careful attention to your body reactions. Record these physical responses.

Identification Exercise for Victims of Enmeshment

- Why do you think _____ holds you so tightly bound to him or her?
- What purpose/purposes does it serve?
- How do you think he/she feels about your independence? Your individuality? Your success?
- What price are you allowing him/her to extract from you?
- Why?

4) Repeat the last exercise for any other person in your life, who holds you under his/her enmeshment sway.

5) In your journal, write the answer to this:
   What would happen if you showed the exercise you've just done to the person? Would he or she rant or berate you? Would he or she feel so let down that the burden of guilt would be palpable? What would your response to this reaction be? Assuming that what you have written is your truth, what would be the worst part about sharing that truth with the individual?

If you think you may have been the perpetrator of the cycle of enmeshment, ask yourself: Are you demanding that others fill holes in you that have been left by not enough love or the denial of permission to define your own self? If so, why do you feel you have the right to demand this? What do you have to lose by allowing others to be whole and free? Do you feel that because of your own unfulfilling life, you must own another? Do you fear that you are in the wrong job or the wrong relationship and that witnessing a loved one grow toward success and happiness would intimidate and threaten you?

Only the brave can dare to look at their responses to these questions. For they are not easy things to even think about, much less admit. Nevertheless, they may be the very things holding you back from enjoying a complete and unfettered life, because when you keep another bound, you too are bound. The love you deeply crave will never be yours, because one who feels owned will never feel love toward the one who imprisons.

Acknowledge your new awareness to loved ones you have hurt. Tell them of your determination to change. In this way you will have begun your part to end the cycle of enmeshment.

Breaking the Emotional Abuse Cycle of Extreme Overprotection

The abuse cycle of extreme overprotection is exceedingly complicated and is as difficult to change as all the other forms of emotional abuse we have been studying, perhaps even more so for many people, because it involves parents who have loved deeply but too much. If you're a child of an overprotective parent, you know that the primary desire has been to protect you from life's difficulties, pain and deprivations—possibly the difficult states of being your parents have endured. But you know, too, that because your parents have cared so deeply, they have cushioned the road too much and given you too much of their energy and focus in the determination to make things easier, better, finer and more fulfilling for you. And if you are very honest with yourself, you now know that you have grown to rely on and look forward to this overprotection.

You know, too, that this type of overprotection has been incapacitating. For you haven't developed the natural ability to handle life's disappointments or developed the confidence to make independent decisions and right your mistakes. And so, predictably, you don't even try. You're scared to really attempt things, because if you make mistakes, you won't know how to correct them. In this process of self-doubt, you either expect to live through a loved one, such as a partner or your own children, or bury yourself in mindless, numbing and unfulfilling activity, afraid to define and search out what you really want.

You may be aware, too, that you have a tendency to expect too much of your friends, your partner or spouse, your work colleagues or employers. When you fail or they react to your demands negatively, you still expect your mommy or daddy—or someone else—to make things right for you.

If part or all of these patterns of action and reaction are a part of your life, determine right here and now to change things. Tell yourself that you can, you must and you will. For the next three weeks I want you to complete the following "homework assignments," after which you will write in your journal about what you felt and did during this time.

Self-concept Exercises for Victims of Extreme Overprotection

1) Do something that will make you happy and that you can accomplish all by yourself. It may be going on a hike or going to see a singer-songwriter at the local concert hall. The challenge should come not from the difficulty of the activity (i.e., don't try climbing Mount Everest!) but in doing something

that you can only rely on yourself for. Maybe you will go out to dinner alone before the concert, negotiate the parking and the directions, determine the timing of the entire evening. After the activity, write about your experiences in your journal. (Yes, in your private space. Yes, aloud—you know why!) If it didn't work out to be all you hoped for, vow to pick yourself up, learn from it and move on. If you truly enjoyed yourself, then plan your next activity!

2) Now take this same spirit of adventure and apply it to some other area of your life: diet, exercise, career choice or dating pattern. What you choose should have a little more at stake; it should be something that has not been working out the way you would like. Brainstorm about why this aspect of your life is not going smoothly. If overprotection has been at the root of it, try to figure out from what you have been protected. Might the answer to your problem lie in a shadowy area which, in spite of fear and anxieties, you must bravely address on your own? For instance, do you remain overweight, because you fear an intimate relationship with someone who doesn't want to coddle and baby you, but would expect a mature relationship? Do you refuse to act as an adult at work or in other settings, because if you can conduct yourself in this way, you will have to stop being bailed out constantly by one parent or both?

3) Parents who overprotect are usually very open to honest communication. If they are not, you've probably misread the cycle and they are really involved in the cycle of enmeshment. Parents in the cycle of extreme overprotection will be upset by your inability to have a more happy life and wish you well. So your next assignment is to talk to them honestly, to tell them that they are there *too* much—they care *too* much—and that they have to back off. Prepare yourself by writing in your journal

what you will say. As usual, read aloud your words in private and note your reactions. Of course, when you actually speak to your parents of this, you will want to note their reactions, as well. You may be surprised—often they will respond with relief. Record this experience and, as before, read it aloud. How do you feel about the conversation and the responses to it?

4) Do this last assignment when something bad happens to you. Hopefully, it will not be a tragedy, but rather a minor setback: a friendship sours, a grade in a course isn't all you wished it to be, difficulty with a job or a member of your family. Note the desire to turn to your overprotective parents. Examine what feelings are too difficult to handle on your own. Why? How will you feel about yourself if you don't turn to them for a bailout? Now consider what your feelings about yourself will be if you do turn to them once again for help. Record your choice and why you made it. Read it aloud, paying attention to the emotion in your voice and your body's reaction.

If, on the other hand, you are the overprotective parent, recognize that you are not helping your son or daughter at all. Tell yourself again and again that loving too much is no gift to your children. Tell them also and apologize for this crippling behavior toward them. Then change it!

If your son or daughter gets sick at college and it's nothing serious, don't rush there with medication. Because in doing so, you are not helping. Instead, you're giving the message that he or she cannot cope with this problem. Following this line of thinking, if an important relationship ends, be there if a son or daughter reaches out to you, but don't coddle him or her. Let your child reach out to friends and others with whom he or she has formed adult relationships. Don't need or expect your child to run home to you for comfort.

In like vein, if your adult children get into troubles at work, express confidence in their judgement to use their abilities and work things out. Tell adult children you expect them to learn to get along with others and be self-supporting. Tell them they can make or break their own lives. It is up to them! In this way, you will have done your part to end the cycle of extreme overprotection.

If your overprotection has led to your son or daughter choosing an individual with a dictatorial personality as a lover or a partner, one who, "always knows how to fix things" as you did, be there for your child, but don't judge. If you are highly critical, that may tie your son or daughter to this person, because he or she can't bear to admit—especially to you—failure once again.

The less you judge, the more your adult children can turn to you in appropriate ways. Tell yourself again and again that bailing sons and daughters out and offering too much caring, comfort and directions does the reverse.

It's obvious that you love your children. Love them enough to curb your strong need to make everything right in their lives. If you do not, you'll accomplish just the opposite. For overprotected children become friends who expect too much from other friends, partners who either expect too much from mates and/or marry dictators, adults who expect too much from their children, employees who cannot get along with colleagues and peers and employers who become tyrants. Or, in perhaps the saddest situations, they become sons and daughters who, in their fear of ever leaving Mommy and Daddy, live isolated and lonely lives.

Breaking the Emotional Abuse Cycle of Rejection/Abandonment

As we've discussed, those experiencing the cycle of rejection/ abandonment learned in childhood that they could not have a feeling, need, opinion or direction that their parents did not approve of. If they said something their parents didn't like, the result was a withdrawal of love, their physical presence or both. This leads such individuals to fears of intimate relationships, to rebellious flings with those who will hurt them, to conducting themselves toward others who care for them in the same manner as their parents did or to perpetuating the cycle they experienced as children by being attracted to partners, friends, work colleagues or employers who treat them in familiar, hurtful ways.

If you have been and continue to be a victim of this cycle, first and foremost, face it. In your love relationships assess whether you can have an honest conversation with those you care about who have hurt or continue to hurt you in this way. If you feel that speaking honestly will not be productive, have an in-depth conversation with yourself. Write down everything that you feel about the other person and situation. Read it aloud to better decide whether you wish to speak to them or whether it would be wiser to handle the impact of the behavior within yourself. It's always best to be able to speak directly with someone about whom you care who has hurt you. However, if the conversation cannot be productive or you begin it and it quickly spirals downward, consider this a learning experience, realizing that you still have choices.

If you cannot talk with someone honestly or change destructive behavior, if every opinion expressed leads to withdrawal from conversation or the relationship, is this really a relationship that can or should continue? If so, how can you adjust your expectations and buffer the times you are together?

For the next three weeks I want you to complete the following "homework assignments," after which you will write in your journal about what you felt and did during this time. And you will (you guessed it!) read it aloud. You know why. Facing yourself and addressing your emotions aloud frees your inner voice.

Changing Self-concept Exercise
for Victims of Rejection/Abandonment

1) Seek out a relationship with someone who will be there on whatever level you choose to start. Ideally, this will be someone who will appreciate your good intentions. Volunteering in a

hospital would be a wonderful way to begin. Some patients will really appreciate your being there and will tell you so. Others may be angry about their own lives and illness; they may lash out at you or refuse to speak to you. But this, too, will be a good experience in withstanding rejection and understanding that the acting out has nothing to do with you personally. Because you've just met them, you can know for sure that their rejection is because of their own sadness, upset and lack of control over what life has brought them and their reaction to it.

2) Make a list of people in your life with whom you have fledgling relationships or associations, but ones that never seem to go anywhere. Look into these situations a little more deeply. Were you afraid of getting comfortable with these people when things really might have been all right? Were you so afraid of abandonment that you decided to abandon them before they abandoned you?

3) One thorny reality to confront is the part of you that may replicate the treatment you endured as a childhood victim of abandonment/rejection. Remember: Those who withdraw from others as a means of control are usually very afraid of revealing deep feelings of shame that render them feeling incapable of mature sharing and meaningful intimacy. By rejection and abandonment, they convince themselves that others have wronged them. In this way, they hide from the parts of themselves that bring them enormous shame.

With this in mind, if you find yourself withdrawing from someone who has an opinion, need or direction different than what you wished for in this person, force yourself to discuss, communicate and keep the dialogue going, rather than allow yourself to retreat into an old, ingrained pattern that caused you so much suffering. Practice these sentences: "I want to understand you better." "Help me understand." "Talk to me and I will listen." "I promise that I will not leave the room or the house while we are discussing this." "I will be there for you." (Aren't these the very sentences you longed to hear from your loved ones when you were a child?) Then listen to what the person says. When, and only when, he or she is finished, respond, beginning with, "I hear you and believe (insert a thought of yours here, not an attack on the other person) or "You have given me something to think about" or "I don't see it that way. Here's what I think." Conclude with, "Let's continue to think about what both of us have said." Remember, practicing makes the strong and mature reaction become more and more likely to be the natural reaction.

4) If you fear putting your new method of listening and responding to use, ask someone you trust to role-play a situation with you. Discuss an argument that would, in the past, make you retreat or withdraw. Practice your new way of reacting.

5) Then, when you are ready, go back to Step 3.

If you have unknowingly or knowingly caused people pain through the rejection/abandonment cycle, learn from it. Will yourself to act differently and apologize sincerely to those you care about and whom you have hurt. Practice your new ways of communicating. In this way you are doing your part to break the cycle of rejection/abandonment that you learned in childhood and have been perpetuating.

Breaking the Emotional Abuse Cycle of Complete Neglect

The case of April in chapter 2 showed that the cycle of complete neglect is desperately painful. Those who have suffered from it must bring into their lives people who are kind and caring as a replacement for the parents who gave and cared so little, if at all. If you have suffered from this cycle, chances are strong that you have avoided relationships or have chosen one with a partner who treats you as your parents did. Chances are also strong that when a different quality of love and caring has been offered in friendship, in love, in the community or in the workplace you either didn't recognize its authenticity or you didn't feel deserving of it.

For the next three weeks I want you to complete the following "homework assignments," after which you will write in your journal about what you felt and did during this time. And you will read your entries aloud.

Self-concept Exercise for Victims of Complete Neglect

1) Speak to yourself *every day* about deserving to be cared for and treated with respect by those who are capable of this quality of mutual respect. Find a mantra that speaks to you and paste it on both your bedroom and bathroom mirrors. This will be an affirmation of your right to live and find happiness in this world. Repeat aloud that mantra to yourself every morning and every evening and know it is true.

2) Keep your eyes open and reach out to people who are capable of kind, quality interaction. It may be difficult, because you are used to overlooking these people due to your belief that you are not worthy. When you encounter positive people either at your workplace or by joining a book club, a cooking class or a discussion group, revel in the humanity of being on even ground with another person. Know that this can occur every day of your life.

3) Consider those with whom you are already in relationships at the same time that you are beginning to reach out. Write in a journal why you do not like the way you are being treated and how much better you deserve to live and relate. Decide if you can effectively talk about the disrespect to those about whom

you have written. If the situation cannot change, recognize that you have options. Equally as important, ask yourself how you are treating others. Record your reflections honestly. Read them aloud. Be honest with yourself. Will yourself to treat people differently than your parents treated you. In doing so, you will break a dreadful cycle and give all you care about, including yourself, a precious gift.

4) Start doing things differently by getting a pet or a plant for which you will care and nurture. Such an activity is a good place to begin. In doing so, you will not only be participating in helping another living thing to grow—and in that way stimulating your own growth patterns—but you will begin to realize what a glorious thing it is to give. That may be your ticket to understanding what your parents missed out on by treating you with neglect. Possibly this will engender your compassion towards them.

5) Begin now to relate to people on a more intimate level. Find one or two people to go to a movie with, share a meal with, not necessarily romantically, although it could be if you're feeling brave. Tell yourself that you are ready to give this person or these people the best that you have to offer and will expect the same from them. Assume—despite the many painful experiences you have had up until now—that this is what will happen. Believe in yourself and you will make this dream come true.

If you've treated someone with the disdain of complete neglect, you have been wrong. The next step won't be the bitter pill you think it may be. Apologize, own up to your mistakes and be available in the here and now. Mark today as the first day in the rest of a very different life. In this way you are doing your part to break the devastatingly painful cycle of extreme neglect.

Setting Myself Free

I experienced the necessity of freeing myself from a repetitive cycle of emotional abuse in adulthood, which derived from my childhood experiences.

After eleven years of marriage, I knew that divorce was necessary. But I believed in marriage and I deeply hoped for another opportunity for love and commitment.

Four years after my separation and subsequent divorce, a couple I knew told me that they wanted me to meet a friend of theirs, a physician named Stan. Giving careful thought to our first meeting, they telephoned him. Without mentioning my name, they told him they wanted to introduce him to someone, but they had two questions: Was he definitely getting a divorce? Was he having a good time dating?

Stan responded that he was separated from his wife for the third time and that for the first time he was dating and enjoying it. However, he couldn't say whether he would be divorced: After each separation he had returned home, because he missed his children so much.

My friends told him that if he decided to get a divorce and stopped enjoying dating, he should let them know. He asked for my phone number, but my friends refused.

Several months later, Stan phoned my friends to say that he was getting a divorce.

"Are you still having a good time dating?" he was asked.

Ever honest, he replied, "Yes." That ended the conversation.

About six months later, Stan phoned my friends again and laughingly told them that if he could have my name and phone number, he would promise to propose on our first date.

One January evening a few days later, as I was reading a story to my younger daughter, Kathyanne, Stan phoned. I asked if I could return his call. Later that evening, after the children were asleep, Stan and I spoke for a long time. He suggested that we go out the next weekend.

I remember checking the telephone book after our conversation to make sure that Stan really existed. He did—both in the white and yellow pages, where he was listed as a surgeon. I copied both numbers in my appointment book. It is strange: Stan and I had not yet met, but we both now believe we fell in love that night on the telephone.

Earlier that week, I had returned ahead of schedule from a New York City holiday with my daughters, Elisabeth, who was ten years old, and Kathyanne, age seven. I had saved money for months and arranged for the least expensive room (two twin beds and a cot) facing Central Park at the Plaza Hotel. Through careful planning, a lot of clipped coupons and French toast for dinner twice a week (which Elisabeth, Kathyanne and I adored!), I bought three tickets for The Wiz, *arranged for a visit to FAO Schwartz (one gift each), and dinner at Trader Vic's. I knew Elisabeth and Kathyanne would love the special fruit drinks with all the trimmings and I was right!*

Unfortunately, Kathyanne woke up on our third day in New York with a bad case of pink eye. When medication made it worse, we returned home. Her pediatrician and the consulting ophthalmologist believed that a new medication would take care of the infection. Kathyanne was a very good sport. It was a blistering, cold day. We did not own a car. The bus did not come and a taxi (an extravagance, but I would have done anything to find one!) was nowhere in sight. So it was necessary to walk home from the doctor's office. I carried Kathyanne as long as I could and we stopped for hot chocolate. As awful as Kathyanne felt, she said that the hot chocolate was "yummy." Then sensing my concern, my little girl told me, "I'll be better very soon, Mommy. Please don't worry."

However, the morning after Stan's call when I woke my daughters, I was very worried indeed. The left side of Kathyanne's face was swollen and the white of her eye was no longer pink, but now a very bright red. I canceled my appointments and rushed Kathyanne directly to Children's Hospital where a pediatric ophthalmologist diagnosed her condition as orbital cellulitis, a potentially life-threatening illness. Kathyanne needed to be hospitalized immediately. As soon as Kathyanne was settled in a room, I phoned Stan to break our date.

For the next few days, I rarely left my daughter's side. Friends and baby-sitters cared for Elisabeth, with whom I kept in contact by phone. Stan phoned me every day to see how Kathyanne was progressing. The antibiotics did work their magic and ten days later, Kathyanne was out of danger.

Stan asked to pick me up at the hospital late that evening for our first date. I looked an absolute mess and because Kathyanne's IV broke down, I kept him waiting in his car for forty-five minutes. Then, when I finally met him at his car, I explained that I had promised to return to my daughter to read her a story. He told me that he didn't mind, that he would wait "as long as it takes."

When I finally returned to Stan after another forty-five minutes, I had to tell him that I had just learned in a phone call from the baby-sitter that my older daughter, Elisabeth, had developed what might be strep throat and that I would have to go home immediately. Stan told me that he would come, too. I explained emphatically that I did not let my dates and my children meet. But Stan said, just as emphatically, "An exception must be made, because you and I are going to get married."

"You have to be joking," I replied.

But Stan said, "No, I'm not," and I knew he was right.

Upon meeting him, Elisabeth explained she was worried that her guinea pig was ill. Not only did Stan examine Elisabeth's throat, but he also examined Curious George's and proclaimed the latter to be in superb health. Later, Stan shared that during the course of his surgical practice the only throats he looked at had been his children's. He also confessed that while he was used to cats and dogs, until that night he had never even seen a guinea pig, much less one's throat, up close.

From the moment I returned to his car on that freezing January night more than twenty years ago, Stan and I have been together. Two weeks after that first meeting, Stan introduced me to his children, Liz, age twelve, and Doug, age nine, and a few days afterward, Stan brought Liz and Doug to my home to meet Elisabeth and Kathyanne for the first time.

That is one evening none of us will ever forget. Stan and I were very nervous. We wanted everything to go well. But our children were even more nervous than we were! Stan had always told Liz and Doug that they would not meet a woman he was dating until it was the woman he was going to spend the rest of his life with. Elisabeth and Kathyanne knew I loved and trusted Stan very much and so did they. They had heard from me how special Liz and Doug were and, in Elisabeth's words, "We just want to like them, too!"

After this, Kathyanne questioned, "Suppose they don't like us?"

Elisabeth and Kathyanne stood at the window waiting for Stan's car to drive up. Liz and Doug walked up the steps and came in the door. The four instantly liked each other. We knew that everything would be all right. One of the very fortunate things in our marriage is that our four children would have been friends wherever and however they met.

Liz, at twelve, was as tall then as she is now. Yet inside of her there was still a darling little girl who was very open and friendly. I felt very lucky to have met her at this transitional age. Douglas was absolutely adorable and within minutes Elisabeth and Kathyanne took Liz and Doug upstairs to meet the infamous Curious George, whose life, they explained, was saved by Stan.

That night at dinner Douglas was so excited to be there that he overturned his chair. The next day we went to the zoo where the four of us invented a game. We looked at the people walking around the zoo and gave our impressions of what kinds of lives they lived. I think we played this game, because all of us were long-ing to come together as one, big, happy family. This game became the way each of us shared our hopes and dreams with each other. It was during that two-day period together that we began to feel we were becoming that wished-for family.

Stan and I were determined that nothing would ever diminish our love for each other and we both found each other's children so appealing and open that our love for them was immediate. We know that such instant love is not always or even usually the case in second marriages and it has been a blessing in our lives.

However, that doesn't mean that the going has been easy. There have been rough times, rough arguments and sad moments between the six of us. It has taken an enormous amount of work from all of us to be a real family. Isn't that the case in every family?

It is difficult and painful to grow up. Though some childhoods are easier than others, none is without conflict. In order to pass from childhood to adulthood, each of us must face very difficult internal and external challenges.

Living with others requires limitations on the self and a consideration of the rights and dignity of others, whether they be our partners, our children, our co-workers, our siblings or our friends. Only those who have senses of their own self-worth and dignity and who recognize the worth and dignity of others are truly capable of love.

The bottom line is that each person has the right to develop his or her self and to live as an individual, not an extension of one's parents—even parents he or she may love deeply.

Gaining self-esteem requires the knowledge that we have the power to make decisions that are in our own best interests rather than choices based upon guilt, anxiety or fear. Through this process we learn to trust our inner voices as our guides, guard against bringing avoidable pain into our lives and achieve what is essential: We set ourselves free and in doing so become trusted and trustworthy friends to ourselves. In the next chapter, you will learn more about how to further this process.

9

Learning to Utilize
the InnerSelf Dialogue

If you ask yourself the right questions, the answers can change your life.

"I've finally learned that I have a choice," one woman told me. "I realize that I don't deserve to be hurting—that I deserve to know what happiness feels like."

You have been reading about how our lives, shaped by our relationships as children, have affected us as sisters or brothers, as friends and lovers, as coworkers, employees and employers. You also have read about the importance of self-respect and mutual respect in any successful relationship. In order to make choices that lead to positive, rewarding, stimulating relationships and lives that are personally fulfilling, you must learn to say *No* to the pain in life that is avoidable. You can do this by calling on the inner voice you have been freeing as you have been reading. That inner voice should be used in a technique that I call the InnerSelf Dialogue.

Your InnerSelf Dialogue is a gift you will give to yourself. Once you begin to use it, you will be able to define and move toward the emotionally satisfying life you have dreamed of, but did not know how to begin to articulate or discover. An InnerSelf Dialogue is a conversation, a personal and private form of communication with yourself. It's a process that you can use to consider choices in everyday life, especially decisions about work, friendship, love and investments of your time. I teach this technique to all my clients and I use it regularly in my own life. In time, its use becomes instinctive. As I sit in my kitchen sipping tea, I think, *I am putting this technique to work for myself!*

Learning to Read the Signals - Preparation for the InnerSelf Dialogue

Talking over a problem often will help you gain perspective and make the right decision, whether you confide in your closest friend or a therapist. However, you may not want to tell anyone about your deepest fears or your biggest problems. You may not have found it possible to express them fully even on paper. In time all of this will change. Go to the private place where you write in your journal or any private space at all and promise yourself aloud, "I can and I will face the impact of emotional abuse in my life. I will do it for myself and my future. I will also do it for the future of those I know and care about now or those I will meet in the future." Say it aloud once again. Then promise yourself, "I can, I must and I will." Notice the sound of your voice. Feel your heart beat. Let yourself cry about past or present pain and lost opportunities. But remember—your life is yours today. It belongs to no one else. You can make it or break it. It is all up to you and the determination you feel.

Once you identify the cycles of emotional abuse you endured and vow to remove them from your life, everything is possible. Again and again, I have seen clients who once despaired about their lives see clearly at long last and learn how to take charge of themselves. Their inner voice guides them through knowledge, experience and feelings. Their intuition serves them well. They now are able to make their luck happen. When opportunities come their way, they do not destroy them; they take advantage of them.

Once you have affirmed your belief in yourself and your determination and are in your private space, I want you to respond to the following statements. They are phrased as a set of "I" statements, with which you will be familiar. Your job is to record the truth of your experiences, by answering "frequently," "sometimes" or "never."

By now you know, of course, that this kind of exercise frees your inner voice. It is also preparation for a very important exercise which follows. This exercise will actually record and define exactly which cycles affected or dominated your early life and how such cycles are perpetuated. Soon you will begin to feel dignity replacing shame. You will be in the process of halting feelings of humiliation from forcing you into a repetition and perpetuation of the destructive cycles in your own life. Soon your emerging sense of humility and accompanying pride will remove you from the category of victim forever. Soon you will learn that the InnerSelf Dialogue Technique, used consistently, can free you from emotional abuse—and free your children as well.

Let's begin the first exercise: Speak aloud and pay attention to the sound of your voice and your physical reaction to the following statements. The goal is not only to open up to the specifics of what is being said and your experiences in life thus far, but to be ready to hear who you are in relation to what has transpired. The goal is to get in touch with your core being so that your inner voice can be freed to be your guide.

Getting in Touch with Your InnerSelf Exercise

	Frequently	Sometimes	Never
I am afraid to let myself admit how I feel.	☐	☐	☐
I invest in relationships that appear troubling.	☐	☐	☐
I am not taking responsibility for my own success and happiness.	☐	☐	☐

Getting in Touch with Your InnerSelf Exercise (cont.)

	Frequently	Sometimes	Never
I expect someone to protect me and/or rescue me.	☐	☐	☐
I expect to be disappointed, so I never allow myself to dream.	☐	☐	☐
I am too hard on myself; I expect myself to be perfect.	☐	☐	☐
I accept humiliating treatment at home, at work or in my community activities, because I believe that I deserve it.	☐	☐	☐
I don't consider all my choices.	☐	☐	☐
I am hypersensitive and take people's reactions too personally.	☐	☐	☐
I strike back inappropriately when I receive mild criticism.	☐	☐	☐
I am afraid to try to change.	☐	☐	☐

Unlike the other exercises you have done, there is no scoring for this particular self-test. I do, however, want you to ask yourself "why" to those responses to questions to which you answered "frequently." Concentrate on the particular statement, the response and your question "why" until it leads to a memory or a pressing concern. Write down these memories and concerns. Read them aloud. If you ask yourself the right questions—and answer honestly—you will gain insights and answers that can change your life.

Assigning Meaning to Photographs of the Past Exercise

Go to your photograph albums and select many photographs that depict various chapters of your life. Organize them: Infancy, Young

Childhood, Adolescence, Teenage Years, Young Adult Period and so on. Place photographs depicting milestones in their appropriate age-related category. These will include your baptism and other religious services held at your birth; your birthday celebrations; your first day at school; your confirmation, birth of a sibling; death of a sibling; divorce of your parents; Bar or Bat Mitzvah; high school graduation; leaving home for college; wedding; birth of your own children; death of a parent; divorce, if this pertains; death of a child and so forth. Separate the photographs depicting the years after you left your parents' home from the years before you left. In the first part of this exercise, we will work only with the photographs from this earlier period in your life. In the second part, we will work on your life as an adult.

Part One: Your Childhood

1) Record your observations of these photographs in your journal. How do your parents appear? What does their body language or facial expressions tell you? How do you look? Are smiles real or forced? Are people natural and relaxed or artificial and posed? Read your observations aloud. Remember to note your physical reactions, the sound of your voice and your body language.

2) List, on separate pieces of paper, the five emotional abuse cycles: rage, enmeshment, extreme overprotection, rejection/abandonment, complete neglect. You now know that more than one may exist in your life. Also, cycles may overlap and become intertwined. For example, as you bravely face yourself and your life, you may see that for you, two cycles—the rejection/abandonment cycle and the rage cycle, for example—were intertwined. Or perhaps you experienced the cycles of rage and enmeshment simultaneously. Any cycle can coexist with any other. There may even be three cycles at work in your world, such as rage, enmeshment and rejection/abandonment.

3) Describe in your journal events you remember that had difficult or traumatic overtones. Remember, milestone events trig-
ger an exaggeration of emotional abuse cycles if they occur
within a family. Read your entries aloud. Note your body language and the sound of your voice.

4) Tape together side by side the five pages representing the emotional abuse cycles. Reread your journal entries. What cycle or
cycles have the photographs reflected? Make check marks or
notations on the pages in a way that best describes the cycles as
they played themselves out or combined in the events you
remember.

5) Think back once again on the chapters of your life as a child.
Remember the day-to-day events. Think back to a typical day
and how family members acted toward each other. Review the
photos of non-milestone events. Remember a family vacation,
family dinner, the reactions as you tried to speak and express
yourself, what it was like as you did homework, etc. Record
these memories in your journal below your remembrances of
milestone events. Read aloud what you have written, as you
have been doing.

6) Identify on your sheets of paper the emotional abuse cycle or
combination of cycles that the photographs and your remembrances reveal.

Part Two: Your Life Today

1) Write the names of each emotional abuse cycle on separate
pages.

2) Look at photographs beginning with your adult life.

3) Record in your journal your remembrances about leaving
your parents' home. Review milestone events and day-to-day
life. How have your parents reacted to your adult choices?
Who are the most important people in your life and how do

you relate to them? Write your responses in your journal, paying attention to your inner voice and body language.

4) Describe in your journal your life today and the treatment of those you love, care about and work with. What do your remembrances and observations tell you? What do the photographs tell you? Record your observations. Read them aloud. Feel your words.

5) Put check marks on the page or pages that correspond to the cycle or combination of abusive cycles you can identify.

6) Study the pages. You have now identified the cycles of abuse you live today, as well as relationships and events that triggered them in your past.

You are almost ready to begin the InnerSelf Dialogue Technique for which the past chapters have prepared you. Congratulate yourself! Do so again!! Your inner voice has been found. Dignity is emerging to replace shame. You are on your way to feeling pride and experiencing humility. You have bravely recorded the pattern or patterns of emotional abuse that pervaded your life and continue to do so. Now you are about to get rid of them!

The InnerSelf Dialogue

Through the years, on several evenings each week I have written in my own journal. In these pages I reflected on the experiences that shaped my life and the lives of my loved ones. These reflections serve as a review of how people, in spite of loss, disappointment and pain, can bring about change and create meaningful and fulfilling lives. This process of reflection resulted in the formation of the following InnerSelf Dialogue Technique.

An InnerSelf Dialogue has five parts:

1) *Stoplight: Resolve; I can, I must, I will!*
2) *Yellow Light: Recognize the Danger of Ingrained Pitfalls.*
3) *Red Light: Stop Ingrained Pitfalls; Enough is Enough!*

4) *Green Light: The Process of Saying Yes!*

5) *Maintaining Your New, Safe Speed.*

Let's look at each part in detail.

1) *Stoplight: Resolve; I can, I must, I will!*

Depending on the emotional abuse cycle(s) you have experienced, for one month tell yourself the following every day.

Rage Cycle

> *If someone is angry with me, it is because he/she cares. I will listen and learn from the expression of the person's anger. He/she is not my _____ , who abused me when I was young and vulnerable. There is no need to retaliate with cruelty. I will guard against treating others as I was treated. I am safe now and I will care for myself and others in a better way than I was cared for.*

Enmeshment Cycle

> *If someone wishes to be close and intimate with me, I will not lose myself if I respond. The days of feeling encroached upon and swallowed up by _____ are over. It is a compliment when someone reaches out to me. I will guard against treating others as I was treated. I can care for myself and others. I am safe. I will grow beyond the way I was treated and share this ability with those about whom I care.*

Extreme Overprotection Cycle

> *I can handle my life independently and don't need _____ to constantly hover and be available to bail me out of difficulty or tell me what to do. If I want advice, I can ask for it. I am competent, capable and worthy. If someone reaches out to me, I will be respectful, not expecting from him or her what I expected from _____. I will guard against expecting and demanding too much of other people. I will not do to others what was done to me. I am safe and will care for myself and be respectful of others.*

Abandonment/Rejection Cycle

If someone is telling me something I don't want to hear or face or I don't like the way it is said, I can express myself without leaving the person or the situation. If someone important to me needs personal space or isn't immediately available, I will be okay. I am no longer the vulnerable child who _____ controlled through abandonment and rejection. I need not lash out in ugly retaliation.

Complete Neglect Cycle

If someone distances him or herself or needs personal space, it does not mean that I am unworthy. I will be fine. I will not run from a give and take relationship. I am capable of friendship, love and productive work. I am worthy of finding and maintaining it. The days of cruel treatment by _____ are over. I will guard against treating others as I was treated. I am safe and will care for myself and others in mature ways.

For the next month repeat to yourself the sentences relating to your emotional abuse cycle or cycles at least once every day. Write the words on a card you keep with you or put them in your appointment book, palm pilot or computer. Reread them during free moments. Make them internal parts of your thinking. In the morning or evening when you can go to a private place, say them aloud. Feel your words. Believe them. After the first month, say the words regularly, but not as part of any schedule. Continue to speak them aloud in your private space. Many of my clients repeat these words before and after recording their regular journal entries. Forever after in your life regard them as promises to yourself—promises you are determined to keep.

Any time you find yourself caught up in an emotionally reactive situation or needing to face or handle making a tough decision or being hurt by someone you love or someone with whom you are in any kind of relationship, the first thing to do is breathe in deeply. Then once again recall the words you have learned which are pertinent to the emotional abuse cycle(s) that permeated your early years and continued to repeat. In doing so, you will regain calm and balance. Next, give yourself additional positive reassurance, the kind you would offer to a loved one. Say to yourself:

> *I'm going to be okay.*
> *I am strong enough.*
> *I will survive.*
> *I can handle this.*
> *I will find the right thing to say or do.*

Add any additional affirmations of support that are right for you, ones that will help you calm yourself in times of trouble while you take stock and determine ways to cope. You may want to write down these "mantras" and any additional ones that feel right and are helpful to you. Keep the affirmations pertinent to the abuse cycles you have identified. Remember, one of the many contributions from Eastern religions is the knowledge that in just sitting down alone with our feelings, breathing in and out and letting a little time pass, we are actually doing great healing work.

2) *Yellow Light: Recognize the Danger of Ingrained Pitfalls.*

Do you often feel locked into attitudes, choices and behaviors even when you know there are wiser, more fulfilling options? No one reaches maturity without needing to evaluate how to adjust certain behaviors in order to achieve more effectiveness and success. Habits are hard to change and negative attractions, behaviors and attitudes adopted as a result of emotional abuse are usually firmly and deeply entrenched.

To see and accept reality can be jolting—even devastating. Be brave and ask yourself: Time after time, do I choose people who don't value what I have to say or who constantly question my direction, my reliability and my strength? If so, is there something familiar about their demeaning attitudes and rejecting behavior? Do I choose the same kinds of emotionally abusive people again and again, trying to gain their love or respect? Work to recognize potential pitfalls that lead to your falling into old, unproductive patterns of behavior.

Are you unable to avoid demeaning experiences in friendship, love and work? Are you afraid? If so, of what? Could it be that you fear happiness, fulfillment, feeling whole, experiencing the respect of others? Is the abuse that has stymied you familiar to you? Do you feel that you can't tell a loved one how you feel and what you need? If so, why? Are you afraid to be free because an emotional prison is all you know and has become more comfortable than you realize? Do you fear that speaking up will lead your partner or friends to abandon you or scream at you, perhaps as you were abandoned or verbally attacked by a parent? Will you sabotage love or friendship now offered, because you fear you are unworthy and you think: *If he or she really knew me, I'd be hated,* or *That person must be horrible; if he or she were terrific, why would I be chosen?* Do you turn away from caring friendships or love, because you fear rejection and are determined to avoid the pain of abandonment by taking control and leaving before you are left? Remember, such reactions are a result of shame engendered by the emotional abuse cycles. You can, however, give them up. They must no longer be part of how you view yourself.

Do you feel sad? When we aren't able to face what saddens us, our sadness only deepens. Have you been taught that it's weak or self-indulgent to give in to fear or sadness? If we remain imprisoned by attitudes like these, we suffer, because we can't admit how we feel to ourselves or learn to express ourselves meaningfully to others.

Do you feel guilty? There are two kinds of guilt, one healthy and one unhealthy. Healthy guilt is a signal that you have hurt someone with inappropriate behavior. Unhealthy guilt is an unrealistic fear that you are not giving enough, not pleasing enough or not being enough.

Do you feel angry? If someone has bullied or humiliated you, it's natural to be angry and it's healthy to acknowledge to yourself how you feel. But where do you direct this anger? Anger is a powerful form of energy and you can put it to work for you. You can use it to confront the emotional pain you feel and to think about actions to take to heal it, escape it and avoid it. The challenge is not to turn your anger inward and not to lash out destructively, but instead to handle your options maturely. It is always better to discuss your angry feelings, whenever and wherever possible. The test of your dignity is not if you are angry—life gives everyone occasion to be angry—but instead, how you choose to handle your anger.

Do you feel that you gravitate to no-win, abusive situations? Is there emotional abuse in your past? As we have seen, neglected children who are starved for affection may become adults so hungry for love that any form of attention is better than no attention at all. Remember, with time, patience and awareness, you can and will learn to recognize warning signals alerting you to familiar traps. Once you are able to identify these warning signs, you can change your responses and move toward relationships and experiences that will be healthier and more satisfying.

3) *Red Light: Stop Ingrained Pitfalls; Enough is Enough!!*

Once you recognize and understand your patterns of attraction to and interaction within emotionally abusive situations, you can change them. Imagine that blinking red lights inside your head and heart signal **Stop!** whenever someone important to you treats you disrespectfully or whenever you are about to choose a person or a course of action that could sabotage your happiness by demeaning, subjugating or using you. When someone treats you cruelly and cannot or will not change, there are choices. You can buffer the relationship and do your best to keep it at a distance. If necessary, you can also end the relationship.

There is something else, however, that is important to bear in mind: No one can hurt us as much we can hurt ourselves. We must learn to live, love and work with dignity and self-respect, sending messages by how we conduct ourselves that we refuse to be abused and that we will be respectful of others. Unknowingly, we may repeat negative patterns from the past or choose abusive partners to punish ourselves for feelings that make us guilty (e.g., feelings of rage toward someone we feel we ought to love unconditionally without ever being angry). Or, rather than working out the anger that we feel, we may choose vulnerable people whom we can hurt. Our own attitudes can blind us to opportunities for sharing and growth until we learn to recognize and break the patterns that do not serve us well, until we learn to believe in ourselves enough to tell ourselves, "*Enough is enough.*" Our only hope, if we cannot change reality, is to change ourselves.

Take inventory. What negative patterns do you see in your attitudes? Here are a few examples of negative remarks that you may be hearing from your inner voice:

> *No one listens to me.*
> *It's probably all my fault.*
> *I feel out of control.*
> *I might as well not even try.*
> *You're damned if you do, damned if you don't.*

You may find it helpful to make a list of negative attitudes and behavior—and persons and situations—that you are determined to leave behind.

4) *Green Light: The Process of Saying Yes!*

Practice saying, "*Yes!*" to new opportunities for friendship, love, success and happiness.

In addition to recognizing negative patterns of attraction and interaction, it's essential to consciously practice new ways of thinking and acting. The more you say *Yes!* to positive choices and trustworthy people, the more comfortable and the more spontaneous this response becomes.

Life is filled with unexpected possibilities for growth and fulfillment and to live well means to accept that life is unpredictable. Those who try to keep their lives too neat—always staying within guidelines that were established for them by others—trade passion and joy for the illusion of control and they die without ever having fully lived. Remember: Chaos is normal, life is messy and control is an illusion! The only things you can control are your own choices, use of common sense, determination to hold on to your dignity and how you choose to handle whatever comes your way.

5) *Maintaining Your New, Safe Speed*

As you consider your choices, surround yourself with your chosen community of friends, loved ones and colleagues, those who will respect the decisions you make about your life and treat you with consideration and thoughtfulness. Think of these individuals as your personal traveling companions on life's journey. Constant attention and planning are necessary to make this a fulfilling and successful progression. It's possible for you to create a circle of intimate and professional relationships based on self-respect and mutual respect, even if you have never experienced such relationships. All that is necessary is a belief in yourself, awareness of the emotional abuse patterns that can sabotage you and vigilance.

Be kind and patient with yourself as you journey forth. Think of your reactive patterns of response to emotional abuse as obstructions and detours on your personal highway. These hindrances have been slowing your journey for a long time and you have grown used to their presence. If you are not watchful, they will have a tendency to halt your progress altogether. Remember that it takes constant vigilance to let go of old patterns. You may have believed that unless familiar patterns were followed you would not be able to survive, thus you were afraid to make new choices and claim your own life.

Now you have learned to see the self-defeating patterns in your life. Now you truly understand how and why the negative patterns formed and you see that they are depriving you of joy, success and fulfillment. In other words, you know exactly what has kept you from undertaking or finding pleasure in your journey.

Having bravely faced the facts of your life, you now know that the only path to travel, no matter how stony, is reality. Just as certain potentials and conditions of a journey are predictable, people and situations are what they are. One cannot change a person or a condition by lecturing or demanding. But love, work and belief in yourself will help you develop the confidence to face your problems and find solutions—in other words, to keep your journey progressing! Even small steps of awareness and confident choices will lead to a more interesting and satisfying journey, marked by personal growth and happiness.

Trust your instincts. Your life experience, knowledge and gut feelings unite to become the inner voice which can lead you in the right direction, not necessarily one that is right for your friends, your parents, your siblings or anyone else. In other words, only you know the elements that are needed so that you can move proudly forward.

For the rest of your life you must will yourself to remember the patterns and reactions that do not serve you well. Determine to change them, holding fast, of course, to those attitudes and behaviors that have led you onward to positive relationships and endeavors. For the place in which you began most likely had good elements in it that you have recognized and upon which you can build.

You now know when and why you developed your own perpetuating cycles of abuse and their self-defeating behaviors and attitudes. "I cannot. Why try?" will be replaced by " I understand. I can. I must. I know how. I will." In other words, you have learned and grown and are ready to embark upon a marvelous odyssey.

Learning from this book is a first step in gaining the necessary tools to discern the cycles of emotional abuse in your life and to achieve beauty and accomplishment in your life. I know I am repeating myself, but please accept my confirmatory words. Remember, there are reactive patterns ingrained in you for which you must be constantly on the alert. For instance, if a good friend does not return your telephone call immediately, this rarely means you are being written out of his/her life. What it usually means is she or he is very busy, caught up in personal or professional obligations and pressures, etc. However, those who endured emotional abuse cycles may feel that a call not returned means a friend no longer cares. Utilizing the InnerSelf Dialogue will remind and rid you of such misperceptions. It will help you remember the ways of thinking and feeling that you must avoid in order to reach a satisfactory, creative future.

To best accomplish this task of ridding yourself of wrong turns, roadblocks and other hazards on the road of life and love, continue to keep reviewing the pages that you have just recently completed. Place special emphasis on those recalling the cycle or cycles of abuse in your childhood and now. Regularly review the photographs, memories and exercises that have brought the destructive cycles to your awareness. Will yourself not to fall back on these old patterns of attitude and behavior!

Also, continue to keep a journal. Take time to write and think about upcoming events and deadlines in your life, especially those with the potential to evoke old reactions.

Write about the experiences, relationships and friendships in your life that need to be strengthened and improved. Recognize when you have stepped out of line and work to understand what triggered the bad reactions. Perhaps a friend asked too much or was hurtful and you responded with rage or withdrawal. Decide if it is best to discuss the situation or overlook it. Perhaps, due to your own blind spots, you misperceived and overreacted. Through this evaluation, you will gain the insight to determine which experiences, relationships and friendships need to be altered or strengthened. In this way, you can improve those with potential, decide which ones are best buffered by the presence of others and determine those that need to be let go.

Positive patterns of thinking and acting need continuing attention even after destructive patterns of behavior are broken. Ask yourself regularly if you are presenting your views and approaching challenges with enough confidence. Each day tell yourself:

- *I am a unique person; I'm entitled to live a life that will fulfill me.*
- *I will find the courage to know myself.*
- *I deserve good things.*
- *I can take care of myself. No one has the right to make decisions for me.*
- *I know there is always a way.*
- *If I cannot find the way, I will change direction and try another way.*
- *If one dream is lost, I will find another.*
- *I will never give up.*

At least once a week, take time to think about what lies ahead for you and anticipate pitfalls. In this way you can plan for positive inter-actions. As you make this process a routine part of your response to life's constant changes, you will be able to maintain your momentum of positive change.

10

Affirming the Results
of Your InnerSelf Dialogue

"As a man thinketh in his heart, so is he."

Otto Rank

Employing the InnerSelf Dialogue, which you have now learned, helps you gain perspective and recognize that you have choices in your approach to life, how you regard yourself and how you treat those you love. Your responses need not be a repetition of or reaction to the emotional abuse you now have recognized you experienced.

Utilizing your InnerSelf Dialogue, you can clear your mind and take responsibility for your own behavior. You can discover how to reach out to others and how to understand the opposite sex (as well as it is possible for any mortal to do so!) You can learn from your inevitable disappointments and losses, recognize your opportunities and savor the moment. Most important, you can use your InnerSelf Dialogue to put your past in perspective, refuse to let it dominate you in the present and clear your vision of your future.

The historian, George Santayana, has written: "Those who cannot remember the past are condemned to repeat it." You now are able to appreciate the wisdom of his words in a way that relates to your own life.

In order to affirm and concretize the results of the InnerSelf Dialogue, I utilize several other techniques: perspective, letter writing, journaling, outer dialogue, dreams and individual, marital, family and group therapy. What these practices can do is make the results tangible, real and inescapable to any of us who may still—even at this late date— be trying to escape the effects and implications of a cycle of emotional abuse.

Perspective: An Important Backdrop for Healing

When someone we love consistently has and continues to hurt us through the cycles of the ingrained, emotionally abusive behaviors and reactions at which we have been looking, time alone will not make our feelings of pain and anger go away. For as soon as we begin to recover from one blow, often another will occur. Finding a way to understand what is happening to us, asserting our determination to change the way we are and will be treated and releasing our feelings is like providing a chimney for our emotional home. Without this "chimney," we may become physically ill and emotionally dead, never seeing our options and forever defeating ourselves. We must face the impact of those who have had the power to imprison us. In this way, we set ourselves free.

This does not necessarily mean that you must speak directly with those who have imprisoned you. It may be that even with the best intentions, it would be counterproductive or too painful to communicate with the person who has consistently hurt you. We discussed this subject in a previous chapter and you may have formed a gut reaction as to whether or not direct communication is what the situation calls for. Only you know for sure. It is often wiser and perhaps necessary that the dialogue remain or at least begin within you. What is important is that your emotional abuse must be faced and felt. This is the emotionally freeing process referred to as "working through." The best way to free yourself of the perpetuation of cycles of emotional abuse is by leaving your pain behind. In this way, new methods of functioning within you are carved, new horizons are seen and new attitudes and behaviors evolve naturally and enduringly.

This is the way to resolve any conflict between you and the person who has hurt you. Such conflicts cut you off from positive patterns of attitude or behavior in the present. Several private exercises will help you with this task.

By now you understand that an individual who has hurt you or the people you love has been hurt himself or herself. If behaviors from generations past are chronically ingrained, there may be no windows of available insight and change open to the person who abuses relentlessly. Remember that such behaviors are all the person knew or knows and even though the words and behaviors may well have been brutal for you, the abusive individual's actions were not really about you. They were a sign of a horrid, untamed malignancy passed from generation to generation without intervention.

Remember that you have choices about continuing relationships in your life, as well as how they will be continued. You can decide if you deem them either necessary or worthwhile. Remember, too, that you have choices about how you will treat others. Above all, view breaking the cycle of chronic, ingrained emotional abuse as not just a gift to yourself, but also a gift to all whom you love.

Letter Writing

By recording our insights and valuable revelations, they become amplified and empowered. One of the best ways to do this is in the context of expressing to others what our individual truth has revealed itself to be.

With this in mind, if may be very helpful to write a letter to the person who has hurt you. This should be a letter that explains how you feel, without attacking or judging anyone else. Write how you feel about what this person has given you, both positively and negatively.

Review your relationship from the beginning, recalling your perception of how events and emotions evolved. Write of your regrets and use this letter to mourn the love and respect you lost or never received. Writing this letter can be restorative. Remember that there is nothing to lose from this process; you need not ever mail the letter or share it with others.

After you complete the letter, go to your quiet private place and read it aloud, letting yourself feel the impact of your words.

Next, write in your journal what you believe the response from your loved one would be if he or she read the letter. Place another chair across from where you were sitting when you wrote the letter and sit in it, reading the words you have imagined coming from this person to yourself. If you prefer, stand and then face yourself, going back and forth in dialogue as you imagine the other person's position and then respond as yourself. The goal is to work toward empathy—the ability to see the world through another's eyes. Try to understand how this person's weaknesses or old injuries could have caused your own injuries. Keep writing and speaking in this back and forth way. Explore changes in family relationships and identify unresolved issues, as you position back and forth. The enlightened perspective of insight and empathy leads to compassion. You will see and understand things in a new way. As in the InnerSelf Dialogue, you will be in the process of setting yourself free.

The insights, empathy and compassion you gain through this new understanding will help you put an end to your frustration, guilt and bitterness and will let you break any negative hold this person may have on your life. You will view your abusive loved one in a new way, one that will enable you to resolve your relationship with him or her—even if this individual has hurt you deeply, even if you no longer remain in contact. To conclude this process, write a final letter to express your new understanding. Keep this letter; it is part of your healing process and a symbol of your inner work.

The Outer Dialogue

When personal contact with a loved one is unrealistic or impossible, another way to resolve feelings of pain or conflict is to imagine that your loved one is seated in a chair opposite you. It is helpful to place a photograph of the person—or a series of photographs from several time periods—on the chair. Sit close by. Tell the person how you have been hurt and ask about the reasons for the way you were treated. Let each photograph on the chair help you to bring back memories of your experiences and how you coped with them. These memories also may help you understand who that person was during earlier stages of life. Think about that person's life: What attitudes and behavior that hurt you deeply may have been a reaction to his or her childhood cycles of emotional abuse and repeated in adult life?

Once you've taken time to reflect on your own life and that of your loved one, take the opposite chair and try to answer your own questions about how you were treated. Some of the "responses" you "hear" may be, "But I didn't know any better." or "I only treated you the way I was treated." or "I never realized how I made you feel." or "I wish I had known better. I truly do." Change chairs. Lose yourself in this exercise. Let your inner voice imagine and be your guide. Then speak.

Visualize yourself as a powerful person. You are in charge of your life. Be thoughtful and let your feelings give your thoughts and words spontaneity, which will lead to perspective and direction. Tell your loved one, "I liked you when _____." or "I loved you when _____." "However, I intend to get rid of _____ (name the cycle of abuse and examples of your pain)!" Release your anger about the attitudes and behaviors that hurt you the most. Be specific. Let yourself feel. Let yourself say things like, "How could you have _____?" or "I hated you when _____."

This process should unfold slowly, through a series of dialogues. Choose a peaceful place where you won't be interrupted and return to the same place each time. Plan to spend at least fifteen minutes in this dialogue, until you can allow yourself to experience your pain and recall the events that prompted it. At the beginning of each dialogue, you may find it helpful to light a candle in order to signal this private ceremony and to symbolize hope.

Remember as you speak that you are concentrating on the deepest part of yourself. Your goal is to locate your pain, understand it and finally be able to release it. Let yourself mourn what you have lost or what you never had. This will be an emotional process and you may find yourself crying. This is positive: All of us who live fully experience times when we break down. In doing so, we let out some of the poisons that impair us from reaching our full potential.

Let your "conversation" and the resulting release of anger and tears rid you of shame, no longer making you a passive victim to humiliation. Remember you are in the process of setting yourself free. Remember you can, you will and you must do it. If it will help you, take a pillow and let yourself pound it (but not hard enough to hurt yourself) as you release your pent-up grievances in this way.

Remember that outward cheerfulness may not be an expression of happiness; sometimes it is only a charade performed to mask pain and to deny the need to mourn. True happiness and real energy come from removing the walls that block your creative expression and cut you off from positive choices in friendship, work and love. And this removal of what imprisons you and keeps you from what you deserve is exactly what our work has been about—exactly what you are in the process of achieving for yourself.

Dreams

Listen to what your dreams are telling you. Write them down and reflect upon them. Once you are using the InnerSelf Dialogue and the related techniques described in this chapter, your dreams may suggest unresolved emotional issues that could be keeping you from reaching your full potential. Some of my clients have dreamed of their parents expressing terrible anger toward them, because they have grown, changed and left old ingrained patterns of action and reaction behind them. Through incorporating your dreams into your Letter Writing and Outer Dialogue, you can often gain insight into whether there may be an opportunity to hold a positive, face-to-face dialogue with a loved one in order to discuss an unresolved problem. Several persons have dreamed of their parents telling them, "I did the best I can; please forgive me. The best of me is with you. And I can understand your need to let go of the worst in me." Dreams like this may be only wishful thinking, but they also may be signals that it is still possible to reach out for direct contact with a loved one who has been hurtful and find reconciliation with that person.

Psychotherapy

Sometimes, because of deep trauma, it's not possible to fully resolve emotional issues through the InnerSelf Dialogue and the related techniques described. In this case, a course of individual, couple, family or group therapy can help to pinpoint the impact of cycles of emotional abuse. This can lead to an understanding of how abusive cycles developed and lead to positive life-affirming replacement of self-defeating behavior and deeply ingrained negative attitudes.

In individual therapy, the client works with a trained therapist, learning to remove barriers that inhibit emotional growth. In marital and family therapy, the "system" at work in the marriage or family can be focused on and any cycles that impede it can be explored and, whenever possible, eliminated. I have grown to view group therapy as a very effective way to confront the impact of the five cycles of emotional abuse and their overlap. With time, every therapist evolves his or her own style of psychotherapy. When I suggest group psychotherapy, I still often recommend some individual, marital or family therapy to augment and enrich the group process and individual growth.

In group therapy, the assembled individuals act like mirrors that reflect each others' emotional landscapes and provide kind but honest feedback about each participant's attitudes and behavior. As weeks pass, the group becomes a community where members can trust one another and speak from the heart. Once members of the group feel safe and are ready to trust others with their most private pain, they can begin a dialogue with one another and with themselves. In this way, they learn to face their grief, mourn, heal, change and grow. Through this process, they learn how to rid themselves of the shame that the cycles of abuse have brought to their lives. They learn how to create a chosen community of their own and how to recognize new opportunities.

In coming to final terms with the past—finishing your emotional homework—you will come to understand how negative attitudes and behavior were born of the shame caused by one or more cycles of emotional abuse in your family of origin. This process will enable you to complete your emotional homework, to examine myriad options for healthy behavior and to identify and locate the path that is right for you. In your daily life, you will begin to hear your inner voice warning you, "Stop perpetuating one cycle of emotional abuse or another and end their accompanying negative attitudes and behaviors once and for all!" The voice will be specific in the "not necessary, can do" department: "It's not necessary to dwell on that any more, to do that anymore, to react that way anymore. I can instead see clearly, understand differently and begin to act wisely, productively and creatively."

Whether you conduct your InnerSelf Dialogue in the privacy of your home or in the office of a therapist, the most effective communication will take place within yourself. Let your inner voice inspire your imagination and propel you to grow and heal. This change within you will help you to move on, create your own chosen community and choose a life that's right for you.

Each day, even a painful and difficult one, gives us something from which to learn. With this new, positive attitude, there truly is nothing to fear. It's been said that each day is a precious gift. Maybe that's why it's called the present.

I have come to a point of realization that I wish for you.

On the last night I dreamed of my mother, I sat on the floor of my kitchen at three in the morning, pages of my journal strewn all around me. As I sifted through the hundreds of pages I had written and carefully studied many times, I was convinced that I had omitted something important.

For a while I imagined my mother watching me silently, a knowing look on her face. Then we began a conversation. I could hear her saying, "What you're looking for isn't written in the pages you're scattering everywhere. You're making quite a mess."

"Stop being such a neat freak," I murmured. "I'm working and you're bothering me."

"The mess is in you."

"What are you talking about? I've been writing this journal for years. It's all here. Everything's here. You're being weird."

I could hear my mother's calm voice saying, "Listen to me. I may be weird, but I know what I'm talking about. What you're looking for is inside you. We have some unfinished business."

"Okay, Mother," I went on, "but so help me, you're being weirder than ever! What business?"

"You know. You really do. It's time for you to face it," I could hear her saying.

"Face what?"

"Your anger at me."

"I don't want to," I responded. "I only want to feel our love."

"Your anger is justified. If you don't face it, it will corrode your soul. We've got to talk about it."

"Why didn't you protect me?" I wondered. "Daddy could be so mean. Why didn't you step in and stop him? I was too young to help myself. You let all the horrors happen."

"How could I protect you when I couldn't find the strength to protect myself?"

"We were both hurt so badly. I didn't know what to do. And when you turned on me in your angry moods, I became so frightened and lonely."

"I'm sorry. I just did not know how to do what was necessary."

"If I had realized how much you needed me, I don't think I ever would have been able to leave home."

"I know. I was jealous of your opportunities—afraid you would leave me."

"Have you forgiven me for leaving?"

"A long time ago. But I know there is something more, something very hard for you to discuss with me."

I started to shake, my voice trembled, my words coming from a place within I didn't even know existed. "What are you talking about?" I asked.

"I'm talking about Louise. It's time to finally talk about her. It's time we talk about that terrible day."

I know exactly the day my mother described. Louise was a woman hired soon after my sister was born to care for us, one of the few kinds of jobs with any dignity offered to an African-American woman in Baltimore during the 1950s when I was growing up. Louise, unmarried, became pregnant and gave birth to a child. When the child was about six, she brought him to visit our family for the first time. The day of the visit, I asked the little boy, who was obviously terrified, what his name was.

Louise responded for her son, "He is Charles."

"Charles?" I asked, surprised.

"Yes, after your father."

My mother went into the house. When my father left to drive Louise home, my mother came into my bedroom and cried uncontrollably. When my father returned, my parents had a horrible argument. My father left the house and my mother remained in her room for hours. When I tried to speak to her or encourage her to eat or drink something, she mumbled incoherently, "Where could I go? Who would care for us?"

Years later, when my daughter Elisabeth was an infant, I became very ill. My mother was concerned, but unable to help me and I could scarcely find the strength to move, much less care for Elisabeth. A few hours into the second day of my illness there was a knock at the door of my apartment. There stood Louise.

"I heard you were sick. I came as soon as I could catch a train."

"Who told you, Louise?" I asked incredulously.

"Your mother told your father to tell me."

"My mother?" I asked again.

"You know I always have loved you and want to help," was Louise's response.

Louise stayed throughout the week until I recovered. I carried Elisabeth in my arms as together we accompanied Louise to the train station.

There Louise clung to me, crying as bitterly as had my mother years before. "Someday you will understand. Don't let people take advantage of you like I always have. Promise me you will always have courage. Promise me you will learn to say 'No' and mean it," she implored me.

"Someday you will understand," Louise kept repeating as she clung to me, stepping onto the train at the last possible moment.

That was the last time I saw or spoke to Louise. I never knew her last name or where she lived. I never asked my father about Louise or her son, Charles. I feared his wrath, but I also felt that any request would be disloyal to my mother. While my mother lived, I never discussed either Louise or her words during her final visit with me in Philadelphia. And my mother never brought the subject up either. That is until this "conversation."

"It's time we talk about her," my mother interrupted my thoughts insistently.

"I can't. It will hurt you."

"You must, please."

"Was Dad the father of Louise's son?" I finally was able to ask.

"I don't know. I really don't. But I do know that Louise was a good woman. She loved you and suffered every bit as much as I did."

"I loved her, too."

"*I know. She was very good to you.*"

"*There's an angry look on your face,*" my mother said. "*You have more to say. Say it.*"

"*The only times in my life I ever saw you happy, I ever saw you smile—were when you were away from Dad.*"

My mother interrupted, "*I would not have left him. The times were so different. There was no place to go. My shame would have been too great.*"

"*Greater than it was?*"

"*Probably not, but I did not understand that then.*"

"*It was awful to see you suffer so. I'm angry that there wasn't time for us—when you could enjoy Stan, the children, our family—when you could have smiled, laughed with us and been happy.*"

"*There's more—say it!*"

"*I'm angry that you never came to see me without him. You missed so much and we missed being with you. Okay, you couldn't leave him. But why couldn't you at least have visited without him?*"

"*I was afraid. I didn't know how to leave my prison.*"

"*What you were really afraid of was being free!*"

"*That's true. I didn't know any other way. I was afraid of his temper. Every time he walked out, I thought I would die. I wish now I had been able to stand up to him.*"

"*And I wish, as much as I wish anything in this world, that he had died first—and then you, Stan, the children and I could have had some precious time together.*"

"*I would have cherished that time also. We would have smiled and laughed a lot together.*"

"*Yes.*"

"*We would have cried, too.*"

"*Yes.*"

I allowed the tears of release to come as my mother's voice continued. "*I have always believed in you and I am proud of you. And you must know that*

I have always loved you. That's why I waited for your birthday to finally let go of life. I wanted to share one more birthday with you on this earth."

It was then, a year and a half after the first time my mother's voice awoke me, that the concluding part of my journal was complete. Our story was written and our work together was finally done.

I am under no illusion: Throughout the year and a half when I heard my mother's voice, she was never alive, never in the room with me. Our conversations and my journal were part of my own InnerSelf Dialogue, a process necessary in order to complete my emotional work. Until I could feel how deeply my mother had hurt me and face my own longing for more time with her, my suppressed emotions would erode my capacity to love others. During her lifetime I had accepted an intense love between us, but I had to make peace with the pain she had inflicted on me.

On the extraordinary morning when I finally realized that I could be fully responsible for my own life, I could sense all of my anger and unfulfilled longing disappearing as my mother's love moved closer and closer toward me, then within me. I could see her smiling face and could hear her words:

"In the end, I promise, every outcome of every problem, every challenge, every disappointment, will depend on your attitude, insight and courage—on your ability to face reality. Your success is up to you.

"The more time that passes, the more you will be able to realize that all acts of kindness, compassion and courage become acts of hope and a gift of endurance to those you cherish."

The personal work between my mother and me was finally completed and our story was before me in the pages of my journal. I could hear my mother's voice, now from within me: *The pain and anger is over and what remains is our love—to be continued.*

Accepting these words, I knew that my mother was now safely inside of me forever and ever. The sun on this morning was unusually bright. A new day! Another blessed, eternal present was beginning.

Unfortunately, not all stories have happy endings and not all problems can be solved. We must learn to endure what we cannot make better, claiming life's joys as we do so and learning everything we can from all that we see and experience.

Use your InnerSelf Dialogue to help rid yourself of the horror that emotional abuse has caused you and will cause those you love if you do not break its vicious cycle. Use it to clear the muddle in your mind as you learn new ways to choose your path and reach out to others. It's not possible to live with dishonesty and not be tainted by it. Face reality: Once you do, you will be able to mourn your losses, complete your unfinished emotional business, change destructive patterns of attitude and behavior and find ways to work things out rather than acting out old patterns that hurt you and your loved ones immeasurably. Only when you understand what is really going on in a relationship can you reach an inner reconciliation. Only then will you know when enough is enough—when it's time to stop hurting and when you have enough self-respect and confidence to live differently and determine the process of healing.

It's never too late for this reconciliation. When we understand and have compassion for those who have hurt us badly, we are free to be ourselves without being hurt by our abusive loved ones. The hold that they once had on us no longer exists: They have lost the power to hurt us. But we can remember that we tried to love them—and perhaps that they tried to love us—and we can see that the love we felt for them is still within us. Knowing this love exists restores our hope for the future.

Believe in yourself. Endure what you must and change what you can. With hard work and perseverance, dreams do come true. If your dream isn't coming true, it may well be that it isn't the right dream for you. The journey you must make to seek your truth can lead to dreams never before imagined. Revel in the journey and let your spirit soar.

Always remember to listen to your inner voice. There is music behind your every word, your every action. Work to understand it, hear its reality and let its truth be your guide.

CONCLUSION

At the beginning of our journey, we discussed the fact that emotional abuse often occurs behind closed doors and that the effects are often invisible. *"The scars are all on the inside, the voice of truth is buried within."* Hopefully after reading this book, if you were a victim of emotional abuse, you now know it. You can't lie to yourself any longer. You now understand that when emotional abuse begins in childhood, it leaves us vulnerable, entrapping us in future relationships with friends, coworkers and loved ones and forming an ever expanding cycle of emotional abuse.

If you were a victim, as you have come into contact with the descriptions of the five cycles of emotional abuse, you have probably been able to recognize more than one cycle which identifies your experience.

1) **Rage**, which can immobilize you and render you helpless to express or assert yourself or render you unable to contain your anger.

2) **Enmeshment**, which leaves you unable to feel and function like a whole and separate person or to choose other whole

people with whom to develop friendships and love or with whom to work successfully. This inability immobilizes you.

3) **Extreme overprotection**, which leaves you feeling (regardless of your academic or professional accomplishments) that you cannot handle the world sufficiently and that no one could ever be as important to you or help you as much as your parents.

4) **Rejection/abandonment**, which leaves you clinging to others, forever fearful of loss—or rejecting people who could offer you fulfillment, growth, contentment.

5) **Complete neglect**, which also leaves you fearful and often isolated and alone, without the confidence to reach out.

Most parents, as I have said, try to do the best they can. The negative patterns that have forced themselves through their lives to be imprinted on yours were created by the generation before them, and so on and so on, back to time immemorial. By extension, not only have you been the victim of the cycle of emotional abuse in your childhood, but you may very well have perpetuated the emotional abuse cycles in each and every one of your subsequent relationships.

First there were your siblings, for whom you may have desired to be the closest of friends, but conflicting expectations and contradictory programming made it all but impossible to share each other's inner feelings, joys and sorrows. Then there have been friends you chose along the way who may have continued the abusive cycle. There were also friends you could have made who would have contributed to your personal unfolding, but you avoided or denied them. Hopefully, you have determined to observe yourself and others with more clarity and reach out to more positive relationships and experiences.

The cycle of emotional abuse you have suffered may, in fact, have affected love relationships you foolishly leapt into and the ones whose call to positive companionship you may not have been able to hear. Or you may now feel even more committed to working on a present relationship after our work together. Perhaps you have recognized a work relationship dynamic resembling that of your family of origin that seemed like an eternal prison, one which until now you didn't know how to escape.

As painful as the process has been, you now know that facing reality is the only way to set yourself free. You may even have seen the way that you carry on the emotional abuse cycle, how your own inadequacy, jealousy and envy can pick up whatever is at hand to bludgeon unsuspecting friends, coworkers and loved ones. Remember, these cycles are organic, they are what is set in place until you put a stop to the range of behaviors that are clearly not serving you or your community of colleagues, friends and loved ones well.

With all this in mind, I have one more exercise for you, the last in this book. So breathe a sigh of relief—I am sure you have our routine down pat by now! Go to a private place and take your journal with you. Respond to these questions: What memories of people in your past stand out as happy and meaningful ones? What people in your present bring you growth and fulfillment? Who are those you want to continue to build with? Who are those you hope to find in the future? Who are those in your present you would gladly—gleefully—leave behind? Who are you ambivalent about? Who are those you want no part of in the future? List the reasons why.

Now again ask yourself all of the same questions replacing "people" with "experiences." For example: What memories of experiences in your past stand out as happy and meaningful ones? What experiences in your present bring you growth and fulfillment? As in the first set of questions, record the reasons for your responses.

After you have written your complete responses and the reasons behind them, read them aloud. Listen to the sound of your voice.

Note your heartbeat and other physical responses. In this way you can put your words and feelings together to hear your inner voice of truth.

Remember that just one recognized, positive relationship or experience helps you to know how to plan for and find others. Throughout life's journey, if you keep your eyes wide open, there will be people and experiences that will help you to put your knowledge, life experience and feelings together and—in spite of many choices and obstacles—consider which ones are wise and potentially fulfilling ways to move forward. Now you know, now you see, now you understand why some of life's major challenges are to know which bridges to work to mend, which bridges to cross and which bridges to burn.

Often a conversation with or a heartfelt letter to anyone who you feel is abusing you can set the record straight and establish new and fertile ground for your relationship. Sometimes, if an individual shows that she or he is not yet ready to make a change, not yet willing to see her or his part in this cosmic dance, buffering is necessary to keep you safe from abuse. And sometimes the relationship must come to an end and you will have to break off contact completely.

Who knows what is the right thing to do? You do. *"The scars are all on the inside, the voice of truth is buried within."* When we first uncover that voice of truth, when it is no longer mute, it may be a yelp or a screech or a crying episode that seems as if it will never stop. In truth, what is happening is the appearance at long last of the inner voice of truth belonging to what the esteemed sociologist and psychoanalyst Otto Rank (a man well ahead of his time) described as the creative force—the artist within all of us. We may not believe what this voice, your inner voice, has to say. Nevertheless, by now you know that the process and intent of this book has been to slowly chip away at your denial and help you to clearly see, feel and identify any cycles of emotional abuse that have imprisoned you. And my hunch is that if you have made it this far in the book, you are at last ready to hear what your true voice has to communicate and you want to help strengthen its message and even out its tone.

Once you know how to recognize the systems of the cycles that may be severely limiting you—once you see the warning signals—then you will know how to stop the patterns of interaction, attitude, and behavior that are not serving you well. You can make the choice to replace them with the things that enrich you, for there is a potential magic light in each of us. When the voice is heard, "the artist within" is able to turn on the illumination.

What can you use to help your resolve to stay true to yourself and to that voice within? This book is one thing. Keep it close at hand and refer to it whenever you feel the powerful negative repercussions of having been a victim of the cycles of emotional abuse coming on. Remember that there are friends and loved ones to trust, a thought which in itself is very healing. There are support groups, individual therapy, couples therapy, family therapy and group therapy which can help you. You also have your journal. In doing the exercises I recommend in this book, you will have many pages of intimate details about times and people in your life, some disturbing, some liberating, but all of them are you, your experience. Do not lose or forget this record of your effort and hard work. Never retreat to your earlier denial that was not helping you, indeed that does not help any of us.

Instead, be willfully determined to make the InnerSelf Dialogue technique an ongoing and natural part of your life. Think of the inner dialogue as your way to understand your own past, one that has been damaged by the cycle or cycles of emotional abuse you experienced in childhood and that continued to limit your potential and harm your vision of future opportunities as an adult. Remember that the cycles of abuse you endured are deeply ingrained. You must be mindful that without vigilance, they will reappear. These cycles are the remnants of past paths, ones that you must no longer tread if you want to reach your full potential. Your new journey is a lifelong commitment.

Above all, remember the power of your own being, of *YourSelf*. If you have remained a hostage to the cycles of emotional abuse that bind you, in spite of the pain they cause you and yours, you know that eventually you must leave this imprisoned state and leave the effects of these emotional abuse cycles behind. You must remind yourself day after day that no one else has the ability to slice through and free you from the tethers of emotional abuse that bind you. Only you do!

You have been learning to hear yourself, know yourself and see yourself as deserving, capable, reliable and worthy of love and respect. Nothing is so powerful, so enduringly beneficial as a good relationship with yourself. You don't have to be afraid that your whole life will change if you truly and comprehensively listen to yourself and plan accordingly. For the change in you, however large or small, is where your inner voice of truth has been trying to guide you.

If you respect your guide, you will experience a contentment, perhaps a joy, that you have never before known. You will be able to find your way out of any maze that is presented to you. And you will learn to live with what cannot be changed in an entirely different way. You will determine to grow from the pain in life that cannot be eliminated. By building your life with those who can be trusted and determining the attitudes, behaviors and reactions that will serve you well, you will not have to undergo much of the pain you now face.

Simply by acknowledging the truth of the situation, you will see what emotional abuse cycles are being propped up like ventriloquists' dummies—where the present is moving its mouth, but it's the past that is repetitively speaking. And you will finally see and take responsibility for changing the damage and ugliness it has caused. As Arthur Miller wrote in the play, *After the Fall*, "The same dream returned each night until I dared not go to sleep and grew quite ill. I dreamed I had a child, and even in the dream I saw it was my life,...and I ran away. But it always crept onto my lap again, clutched at my clothes. Until I thought, if I could kiss it, whatever in it was my own, perhaps I could sleep. And I bent to its broken face, and it was horrible...but I kissed it."

Through this process of facing the truth of your life, however painful and seemingly ugly, you will be able to create a chosen family of loved ones and friends and a chosen community for yourself that is balanced, accepting, fulfilling and rewarding. You will see and understand things with clearer vision. You will move forward with deeper insight and empathy. You will endure with more equanimity; you will understand and be more in touch with and expressive of your emotions. Sometimes you may find yourself taking a step back and simultaneously laughing and crying at life's mad contradictions. This is a perspective you can achieve and move forward. I know. And I believe that you will, as I have.

Please think of this book as a friend—as part of your community. Use it. Plan with it. Keep it with you until whatever parts of it you found helpful are part of you. Use it to conquer your demons and chart your new course. Plan with it to make your dreams come true. And if you find that these dreams just cannot, will not happen, accept that they were the wrong dreams for you. Find others that you can make happen. Will yourself to do so and, despite everything, promise yourself that you will never give up. Say Yes to life. Live.

Always remember that facing reality, no matter how stony its path, is the only path that can free your present and future, and the present and future of those you love, from the perpetuation of emotional abuse. It is the only path to walk upon and build upon. It is the one that can truly set you free.

The Sabbath
of Domestic Peace

"...and among His signs is this, that He created for you mates from among yourselves that you may dwell in tranquillity, and he has put love and mercy between you..."

—Holy Qur'an 4:135

One of the major complications of emotional abuse in relationships, according to recent studies, is its escalation into physical abuse. Nearly one of every three women in the United States experiences at least one physical assault by a partner during her adulthood (American Psychological Association [APA], 1996). By the most conservative estimate, one million women in the United States suffer nonfatal violence by an intimate each year (Bureau of Justice Statistics, 1995); by other estimates, four million women suffer a serious assault by an intimate partner during an average twelve-month period (APA, 1996).

Some years ago, my professional work in consulting with the Sexual Assault and Domestic Violence Unit of the Philadelphia District Attorney's Office, together with my personal experiences, stimulated an idea that I had been developing for many years. Through the years in my clinical practice as well as my community efforts with victims of abuse, I have seen that the majority of abused women first turn to their priests, rabbis, ministers or imams.

Religious leaders are seldom trained to handle the ramifications of domestic violence. Often they do not recognize a cry for help from one of its victims, especially when the message is delivered indirectly by a woman who confesses that things are not going well at home. Sympathetic religious leaders who recognize that these women are in distress—or even danger—more often than not counsel them to go home, try harder to get along with their partners and pray.

I realized that clergy were "the missing link" in addressing the virulent epidemic of domestic violence and that in order to eliminate it, it was necessary for them to be involved in the ongoing, integrated efforts of lawyers, social workers, police, physicians, mental health professionals, agencies and volunteers committed to change.

In 1995, I was instrumental in founding a coalition in the Philadelphia region called the Sabbath of Domestic Peace. This is an interfaith, multidisciplinary coalition of individuals and groups organized to educate and promote discussion among religious leaders and their congregations in order to prevent and reduce domestic abuse.

Many women believe that their religious faith commits them to marriage "until death do us part" and the ideal of forgiveness may prevent them from holding their partners accountable for physical or emotional abuse. Women may feel that they have nowhere to turn for help and many fear that separation from their partners would cause them to be ostracized by communities that have deep meaning to them and their children. Often women think that no one will believe their partners capable of abuse, especially if the abuser is a popular, prominent member of his congregation, as is sometimes the case.

When religious institutions are knowledgeable about domestic violence and when they address this problem openly with their congregations, they can be powerful resources for both the abused and for abusers.

The Sabbath of Domestic Peace is a series of worship services, discussions and other community events that take place each October during National Domestic Violence Awareness Month. It was launched in 1995, with efforts that culminated in workshops, meetings and hundreds of worship services throughout the Philadelphia area.

The first year, organizers of the Sabbath sent more than a thousand letters containing information about domestic abuse to Catholic, Protestant, Jewish and Muslim religious leaders, encouraging them to observe the inaugural Sabbath of Domestic Peace by speaking from their pulpits and by participating in programs and discussions. Events were sponsored by the District Attorney's Office, the Philadelphia Council on Human Relations, the Philadelphia Police Department, mental health professionals and many other civic groups and social service agencies.

As a result of these efforts, Philadelphia became one of the first regions in the country to address the issue of domestic abuse through coordinated, continuing action by houses of worship and communities of faith. Since then, through word of mouth and grassroots organizing, many more people representing a rich diversity of religions and occupations have joined the effort each year. This coalition, once a group of strangers of different faiths, professions and lifestyles, has become a group of friends joined in a continuing dialogue about our differences, with a shared vision of the similarities and hopes which far outweigh them.

Each year the Sabbath of Domestic Peace has been sponsored by a religious organization: The American Jewish Congress in 1995; the Episcopal Diocese of Pennsylvania in 1996; the Presbytery of Philadelphia in 1997; the Philadelphia Baptist Association in 1998; the Board of Rabbis and Young Women's Division of the Jewish Federation of Greater Philadelphia, 1999; the Southeastern Pennsylvania Synod of the Evangelical Lutheran Church of America in 2000; and the Eastern Pennsylvania Conference of the United Methodist Church in 2001.

Each year for the last several years, a prayer and interfaith service has been held for all who want to attend. For several years copies of an informational booklet, *Making Changes, Bringing Hope*, have been distributed to houses of worship, faith communities and the many organizations that have requested them throughout the greater Philadelphia region.

Because a religious leader is often the first person to whom a woman will confide a problem of emotional, physical or sexual abuse, the clergy has a unique opportunity to offer support, crisis intervention and referral. The Sabbath of Domestic Peace has provided these guidelines to help members of the clergy respond to victims of domestic abuse:

- *Listen*. It is very difficult for a victim to acknowledge domestic abuse and a woman may not use the word abuse to describe what happens to her at home. Instead, she may say that her partner is upset or that things at home are not going well.
- *Believe*. A victim of abuse needs your trust.
- *Communicate*. State that no one deserves to be abused. Express your concern. Explain that help is available.
- *Refer*. Provide information about local and national resources. Consider recommending individual counseling, but do not suggest couples counseling, because this can be dangerous while abuse is active.
- *Respect privacy*. Do not contact the abuser without permission; this could put the victim in danger.

When I was growing up, in the late 1950s, domestic violence and emotional abuse were not spoken of within my own religious congregation. But, of course, my mother was the victim of both and so was I.

In those days, when my family lived in Baltimore, we had the most wonderful rabbi imaginable, Dr. Uri Miller. His kindness to me, as one of his students, remains an endearing gift of love that has continually brightened my life and given me strength in my darkest hours. Although he was an Orthodox rabbi, he made a radical statement by allowing his female students to experience Bat Mitzvah and he was a bold civil rights advocate who was chosen to give a closing prayer at the March on Washington led by Dr. Martin Luther King in 1963.

It is Rabbi Miller's views of Judaism that I have tried to pass on to my four children: It is never acceptable to be unkind, ungrateful or without the capacity for mercy. He also taught that someone who sees a wrong and does not speak out is as guilty as the person who inflicts the wrongful act and someone who sees another in need and does not respond turns his or her back on God.

Rabbi Miller, who strictly observed Orthodox Jewish dietary laws, counseled that if one were invited to be a guest in a home and the host served only food you were forbidden to eat, one should eat the food, rather than offend a well-meaning host. Rabbi Miller taught that God would understand.

Yet, as kind, astute and sensitive as he was, Rabbi Miller was fooled by my father's exterior charm and good looks, as were the members of our congregation. My mother and I acted our parts of a happy family with conviction. We were terrified not to. No one dreamed of the actual realities of our lives—how it really was when our masks were off. As I listened to Rabbi Miller's regular sermons, I hoped that he would speak about how wrong it was for a man to terrify his family members and treat anyone the way my father treated my mother. I didn't know what words to give to my father's actions. Today, I know the words are emotional abuse.

But to my knowledge Rabbi Miller never spoke against emotional abuse. I'm sure he never dreamed such a thing could be going on among his congregants. Had he realized, I know that he would have spoken. I know, too, that the power of his words would have given strength to my mother and me.

My childhood had been seared by my father's angry words bellowed to my mother. By the time I reached adolescence, my mother's humiliation had reached the point that she rarely left the house. Her illness would be diagnosed today as agoraphobia. But I will always see it as the death of hope.

Later, when my mother became ill with cancer, in spite of her pain and agony that I witnessed, she still managed to buffer my father's evil. It wasn't until the very end of her life that I understood completely and clearly the extent of my father's capacity for duplicity and cruelty. In her final months and their aftermath, I saw more clearly than ever why throughout her married life my mother absorbed as much as she could bear and took the rest out on me. She knew that I loved her and she trusted that somehow I understood that her outbursts occurred because she hurt so very much. And on some level, she must have known that her love gave me the strength both to understand and continue to reach out to her.

On the day my mother called to ask us to come to Florida, because her death was near, my husband, Stan, and I arrived on an afternoon plane together with our children. I was moved by my mother's bravery, knowing that she telephoned against the wishes of my father. My father made it impossible for my mother to take me to their safety deposit box to give me the things she had saved for me, Stan and each of our four children. We could not reason with him and my mother responded by screaming at him for leaving their bedroom the moment she was diagnosed with cancer and never again returning, not even to hold or comfort her in the dark of night. This was the moment I also learned to my horror that, as ill as she was, my father left her alone in the bedroom for hours without checking on her and sometimes even ignored her when she called out for his help.

Stan and I calmed my mother and said that going to the safety deposit box was unimportant. The important thing for us was to comfort her and be with her. My mother asked Stan and me to take her to our hotel room where she would be able to lie on a bed and watch Al Pacino in the film Scent of a Woman. *How my mother loved Al Pacino! She saw every film he ever made and afterward always exclaimed, in her most Southern accent, "Isn't he just wonderful!"*

During my mother's first bout with chemotherapy, I had taken Elisabeth to a New York City matinee to celebrate her birthday. We were together in the lobby of a Manhattan theater just before curtain time, when in walked Al Pacino. I could barely contain my excitement and couldn't wait to tell my mother. When I called her, she wanted to know absolutely everything:

"What was he wearing?" ("I could only see his coat and a wonderful white silk scarf.")

"How tall is he?" ("Shorter than he appears in the movies.")

"Who was he with?" ("I couldn't see.")

"Some detective," my mother joked, then added in a most serious voice, "How sexy was he?"

"What's the scale?" I asked.

"One to ten."

"Over a million! Absolutely off the charts!"

"I knew it," my mother exclaimed. And then came her oft-repeated line, "Isn't he just wonderful!"

As I have grown older, so many things become clearer. For years, every time I made a connection with a troubled client who then moved forward—learning to say No to self-destructive attitudes and behavior, and Yes to a new vision—I found myself looking up after the client left and tears fell. In recent years I realized that in my heart I was saying to my mother, "I wish I could have helped you, too. I love you."

Throughout my life my father's raging words were weapons directed against me, as they were against my mother—even after I left home and became an adult. Time after time, my efforts to stay in touch with him were rebuffed. Contact with him subjected me to verbal insults alternating with stony silence and placed me in the impossible position of being pitted against other family members.

The emotional abuse I had endured from my father for so many years— his indifference, his humiliating insults and his rage—destroyed all hope of rebuilding our relationship and it also contaminated my relationship with my mother. Nevertheless, in the last years of my mother's life, she and I found ways to reach out to one another, despite our own guilt and anger.

During my mother's final months, she entered a hospice to die and I went to Florida to be with her.

One afternoon I stood by her bed holding her hand. The cancer had erupted everywhere, but her heart remained strong. My mother opened her eyes, squeezed my hand and whispered, "I love you with all my heart and soul."

I thanked her for giving birth to me and told her I adored her. I reminded her of seeing Al Pacino in the last movie we watched together. "He'll win an Academy Award, I just know it," I told her. Our eyes glistened.

I repeated what my daughters told her when they saw her ten days before, "The first granddaughter will be given your name, Charlotte." She smiled. Her face had remained exquisite. A few days later, on the morning of my birthday, she died.

A few weeks afterward, Al Pacino won the Academy Award for best actor. As I watched him accept the award, I could hear my mother's jubilant voice——in spite of death, in spite of cancer, in spite of it all——and I burst into applause and exclaimed in my most Southern accent, "Isn't he just wonderful!"

After my mother died, my father and I spoke less and less. One day, after my father brutally berated me over the telephone as we discussed my daughter Elisabeth's upcoming wedding, I realized that no matter how hard I tried, his feelings of hostility toward me and this pattern of rejection would never change. All my life, despite everything, I had been a good daughter to him and I had never stopped hoping that he would one day be kind to me. But on that day, I decided that enough was enough. I have not phoned him again. Since I had always been the one who called, after that conversation we have never again spoken. Neither he nor my sister attended my daughter's and son-in-law's wedding, an occasion that I know would have brought my mother unimagined joy.

Had my father grown up in a safe and stable home, he never would have behaved the way he did. But try as I might, I could not ignore or buffer myself or my children from his hostility. Finally, I accepted a bitter reality: My father did not want me and everyone I loved in his life. Though difficult at first, eventually recognizing this brought calm and healing.

In acknowledging my father's subconscious wish, I was able to understand that he was not strong enough to face himself, to be accountable for his actions and to give and receive love. At last, I was able to feel very sorry for him, realizing that in his eyes I would ever be a reminder of what he could not acknowledge: what he did to my mother and what I refused to allow him to do to me.

One late summer evening seven years, three months and nine days after my mother's horrible death, my father, I am told, died peacefully and unexpectedly in a favorite chair. He simply fell asleep and never again awakened.

My father was buried in a Baltimore cemetery next to my mother on a lovely summer day. I would like to believe that in some way during these years since my mother's death, he came to understand what he had done to her—and perhaps why—and found peace. I would like to believe that their souls met and that the growth in my father made their reunion sweet.

At the beginning of my father's funeral service, Stan pointed out a lone bird, a Baltimore oriole, that sat very quietly on the branch of a tree very close to us. She seemed to be looking down on us all.

Rabbi Miller, our old and beloved counselor, had been dead for many years. I brought the Bible that he had given me on my Bat Mitzvah day and asked the rabbi conducting the service to bless our four children.

At the conclusion of a Jewish burial service, family and friends are asked to place soil on the grave of one who has died. As I placed the soil on my father's grave, I prayed and silently told him how sad I felt that I had never been able to reach him. I told him that I knew if he had not suffered so much, he would have been kinder to my mother and to me. I told him that I had made a very good life and I hoped he had finally found peace and would be united with my mother's soul.

Later my husband told me that while I prayed at my father's graveside, the lone bird began to sing softly and soon after it flew away.

My father died eighteen months after my daughter Elisabeth and son-in-law Russ were married. His death came less than a year before the birth of a granddaughter who bears my mother's name.

To become content with life, it is necessary to give up the fantasy that we somehow could have changed the attitudes and behaviors of those people in our past whom we loved dearly and needed desperately. Change was up to them. It is necessary to accept that people we loved and relied upon made mistakes, ones that may have hurt us deeply—and it is also necessary, for the sake of our own peace and happiness, to try to understand their actions, to chart a new course for our own behavior and in this way to understand and forgive them.

With hard work, it is possible to soothe the pain that our loved ones, through their own limitations, imposed upon us. And in this way, when love is available, it is possible to claim and keep it with us always. When you possess self-respect and can express respect for others, love can never be lost and is continued forever. Nothing—absolutely nothing—can destroy it. This quality of love is life's only enduring magic.

As we plan our interfaith services for the Sabbath of Domestic Peace each October, I find myself silently saying to my mother, whose great-granddaughter, Charlotte Rose, is as beautiful as she was and has the freedom, love and opportunities my mother could only have dreamed about, "This is for you."

Glossary of Terms Used in *Setting YourSelf Free*

Buffering – Creating a space, the proper distance, between yourself and one who has emotionally abused you. The buffer serves three purposes: it prevents you from further harm until you are able to stand on your own; it enables you to find a new way of living, one free of emotional abuse; and it helps you decide whether the relationship can be salvaged or whether it is too counterproductive or painful to be continued.

Community – There are two pivotal communities in a life experience: that which we are born into and that which we create for ourselves. In a history relatively free from emotional abuse, these two groups can intersect widely and mingle spontaneously. Where there has been a legacy of emotional abuse, however, it is important to assess the community we inherited in order to see if it is the most productive place for us or how it must be changed so that it feels right to us—i.e. a place where we can be accepted and grow.

Compassion – If you have been the victim of emotional abuse, this can be an elusive concept until you realize that your abuser has just been continuing a long line of emotional abuse cycles, over countless generations. If seen from this angle, then *you* get to be the lucky one, *you* get to be the one who learns how to do things differently—and who in turn gets to enjoy the real flowering of intimate relationships with siblings, friends, lovers, workplace companions and community members.

Complete Neglect – An emotional abuse cycle where the victim may have had his or her basic needs, such as food and clothing, met, but in which there was never a feeling of emotional closeness or effective mirroring between child and parent or caregiver. In the absence of any substantive conversations, a victim of complete neglect often manifests very little sense of purpose or any semblance of calm or self-acceptance.

Courage – The resolve and the commitment to know ourselves and to see our own journey through. Without courage, it is not possible to say *No* and *Yes* appropriately, nor can we leave our parents and claim our own authentic, purposeful, passionate life. Courage says, "There is always a way, even if I must change direction." Courage says, "I will never give up."

Cycle – A cycle is something that repeats with fresh material: the form remains the same, while the content has changed. Emotional abuse occurs in cycles, meaning it is "natural" and understandable that it would resurface in similar situations during later generations. The cycle of emotional abuse continues until someone shows the dignity, courage and awareness to identify it and choose differently for himself or herself – thereby breaking the cycle.

Dictator – Dictators can come in two forms: the benevolent dictator, who is basically a kind person whose insecurities cause him or her to become tyrannical or withdraw completely if feeling threatened; and malevolent dictators, who are thoroughly vindictive and who dominate through humiliation, badgering, refusals to hear the words and thoughts of another and by threats of abandonment. Every dictator has two two faces to keep others on the defensive: the Bully, the face of anger and condemnation most often seen, and the Baby, who is prone to temper tantrums, blaming and episodes of sulking and withdrawal.

Dignity – A sense of self-worth, that lends purpose and joy to living. Dignity requires the development of standards, ideas, ethics and responsibilities, as well as the ability to stand off and evaluate oneself objectively. In order to maintain one's dignity or to develop it if emotional abuse has set in, it is necessary to be able to stand up for oneself.

Emotional Ostrich People – Those who have a vested interest in wearing blinders and not facing reality; therefore, all who have contact with them are put in the position of treating them as emotional cripples.

Enmeshment – An emotional abuse cycle in which the family is expected to be one enormous entity, with no boundaries separating individuals—instead relentless togetherness and joint interests are commanded—in order for abusers to feel safe and secure. Sometimes difficult to detect because "the scars are all on the inside," enmeshment can nonetheless have terrifying consequences. Victims are hampered in their abilities to learn to think or act independently. They fear that any normal separation process will mean death—of their parents and themselves.

Extreme Overprotection – A cycle of emotional abuse involving the parental compulsion to protect children from all of the difficulties of life, rather than to allow them to face life's realities and, in doing so, be strengthened. The result is adults, often well-educated and accomplished, who feel crippled without constant parental support. Like those enmeshed, they fear that any normal separation process will mean death—of their parents as well as themselves.

Friendship – Our friends who love us truly and deeply give us the strength to believe in ourselves. Friendship is a flow based on self-respect and mutual respect, not a demand or a stopgap to fill the absences, pressures and pains that we have experienced. We can choose our friends.

Guilt – There are two kinds of guilt: one healthy, the other unhealthy. Healthy guilt is a signal within that you have hurt someone with inappropriate behavior. Unhealthy guilt results in your becoming unable to motivate productive behavior and attitudes, due to the fear that you are not being enough, you are not giving enough, you are not pleasing enough or you are not doing enough.

Humiliation – Humiliation comes from the outside, shame from the inside (see definition of Shame). Humiliation is the tearing down of another's capacities, which leads the person to an inability to assess persons and situations accurately. One who lives in a constant state of humiliation and shame loses the power to assert one's self and insist upon different treatment.

Humility – Recognition of your own limitations, in the sense of knowing what you do not yet know and cannot accomplish or may never know or understand and acknowledgment of how slowly we may have to go to get where we hope to be. Humility is doing our best to accept and endure what this journey of life requires of all of us.

InnerSelf Dialogue – A conversation with YourSelf, a personal and private commitment to yourself. The InnerSelf Dialogue has five parts, which are: resolving to start doing things differently; recognizing the danger of ingrained pitfalls; stopping ingrained pitfalls; saying "Yes" to life's joy and opportunities; and maintaining an emotional home through constant attention, planning and a renewed ability to make positive choices.

Inner Voice – That "still, small" voice which is freed by the InnerSelf Dialogue and which helps guide us toward positive experiences and warns against destructive and abusive ones. In emotionally abusive homes one learns to push down this voice, to stuff it, refusing to hear its message of truth. Over time and through effort we learn to hear our inner voice—the voice of our unique selves—an accurate guide for direction in life and for developing wisdom and courage, as well as understanding life's poetry. Note: If we find that our inner voice says frightening things to us, that is a sure sign that emotional abuse probably has taken place. Frightening and destructive messages mean that you must consult a therapist. Your physician or a friend who has had a positive experience in therapy are good resources for referrals.

Interdependence – The capacity to be respectful, interactive and collegial in love, friendship and work and in doing so achieve a higher quality of fulfillment and accomplishment than one can achieve alone. Like Love, Interdependence is an art form.

Love – Falling in love has everything to do with our past. Love has everything to do with our present and our future. Everyone longs to fall in love and live happily ever after—this is accomplished by being able to shift from being "in love" to "loving" another, to care about your partner without expectations or impositions. The icing on the cake is to be able to maintain the thrill of being "in love" during precious moments and hours within a loving relationship.

Maturity – To be able to be alone, without being lonely; to be able to give, without strings; to be able to work effectively and creatively; and to be able to love are the signs of maturity. For each of us to reach maturity, we must separate from our parents and learn to stand on our own. We must learn to cope with the complexity and challenges of the world without our parents to constantly cushion us. And then we must decide which, if any, of our families' expectations and goals for us are the right ones.

Mental Health – The cornerstone of mental health and emotional resiliency is an inner sense of dignity and self worth.

Pain – Internal pain is a signal that something is hurting you. While allowing yourself to feel pain is a sign of hope and resolve—to listen to what is demanding to be heard. There are two types of pain: that which is unavoidable, like the death of a loved one, and that which can be eliminated, such as being used and treated rudely by friends. Part of life's challenge is to endure and resolve to grow from the pain in life that is unavoidable and to leave avoidable pain behind you.

Parental Emotional Abuse – Each time a child is emotionally abused, the pain—and anger—is buried within. Each event creates a need in the child to either endure or inflict pain. Similarly, each act of empathy, compassion, patience and tenderness enhances the capacity to share respectfully and lovingly with others.

Patterns – Every child reacts to the pressures and conflicts of family life by developing individual patterns made up of habits, attitudes and behaviors. Even though these patterns may be negative or disruptive, they are put in place to help bridge the gap between the child's own desires and the expectations expressed by his or her parents. Once you realize and accept that you have suffered emotional abuse, you can say *No* to perpetuating self-destructive or outmoded patterns that no longer serve you.

Performer – An individual who is fixated on appearances, on how his or her family or marriage or workplace appears and how it is presented, rather than how it actually is. Performers keep as busy as possible, but by never facing the true state of their self- knowledge or their relationships, they risk damaging their physical and emotional health and they reduce much of the potential fulfillment and opportunity for creative expression that life has to offer.

Rage – A cycle of emotional abuse in which anger permeated the victim's home to the point where she or he became unable to think clearly, to trust individual capacity for appropriate judgment or create interdependent and independent paths. An emotional abuser in the rage cycle needs his or her outbursts to achieve a sense of power, control and domination over others, leaving a victim of the rage cycle ill-equipped to deal with the legitimate emotional reactions of others.

Reality – Life without guarantees, without preconceptions, without controlling others is a condition in which the cure can feel worse than the disease. And yet, for those who want to understand their lives, to exorcise their demons and make necessary vital changes, reality, though a long and sometimes brutally stony road, is the only path to take.

Rejection/Abandonment – An emotional abuse cycle whereby parents withdraw their love and affection if a child voices an opinion or manifests a behavior outside the family code. In this cycle, love is shown to children only if they agree with their parents completely, if they "see the world through their eyes." Understandably, the child comes to view love and control as one and the same thing, trusting neither.

Shame – Shame comes from the inside, humiliation from the outside (see Humiliation). Shame is the belief that you have an inborn, built-in weakness or inferiority—are less than, unworthy or unlovable. Those who experience shame feel diminished and that their weaknesses will be exposed. They will try very hard to run from both facing it personally as well as having others see it. Those who live in a constant state of shame lose the capacity to assess people and situations accurately, as well as the power to assert themselves and insist upon changed behavior. All children feel shame to some extent (questioning one's inner capacities is part of growing up). To diminish its effects, children must know that they are loved and accepted and must develop pride in themselves and their origin.

"Sponge" People – Those who drain you of all your strength, leaving you limp and weary. Desperate to be emotionally "fed," these personalities have a difficult time maintaining friends or partners.

"Swiss Cheese" People – Those who ask or demand that others be on constant call to fill in the "holes" and emptiness in their lives.

Warrior – An individual who yells and screams in a constant state of acrimony and ridicule, hurling words and sometimes objects without ever fully understanding the reason for his or her rage. Though there is physical release through verbal abuse, there is no self-understanding and thus no occasion to heal or create intimacy with another. The warrior is largely the propagator of the rage cycle of emotional abuse, but his or her tactics can lead to other cycles or their combination.

Withdrawer – An individual who expresses anger by refusing to speak, sometimes leaving the room or the home or, alternately, by joking, teasing or changing the subject about issues he or she is too frightened and uncomfortable to discuss. The withdrawal of love and affection during emotional exchanges is a brutal and devastating attack on one's family and friends. The withdrawer is usually the propagator of the neglect and the rejection/abandonment cycles of emotional abuse, but his or her tactics can lead to other cycles or their combination.